RECOGNITION IN MOZART'S OPERAS

RECOGNITION
IN MOZART'S OPERAS

Jessica Waldoff

OXFORD
UNIVERSITY PRESS

OXFORD
UNIVERSITY PRESS

Oxford University Press, Inc., publishes works that further
Oxford University's objective of excellence
in research, scholarship, and education.

Oxford New York
Auckland Cape Town Dar es Salaam Hong Kong Karachi
Kuala Lumpur Madrid Melbourne Mexico City Nairobi
New Delhi Shanghai Taipei Toronto

With offices in
Argentina Austria Brazil Chile Czech Republic France Greece
Guatemala Hungary Italy Japan Poland Portugal Singapore
South Korea Switzerland Thailand Turkey Ukraine Vietnam

Published by Oxford University Press, Inc.
198 Madison Avenue, New York, New York 10016
www.oup.com

First issued as an Oxford University Press paperback, 2011

Library of Congress Cataloging-in-Publication Data
Waldoff, Jessica Pauline, 1964–
Recognition in Mozart's operas / Jessica Waldoff.
p. cm.
ISBN: 978-0-19-515197-8 (hardcover); 978-0-19-985630-5 (paperback)
1. Mozart, Wolfgang Amadeus, 1756–1791. Operas.
2. Opera—18th century. I. Title.
ML410.M9W23 2006
782.1'092—dc22 2005006672

Printed in the United States of America
on acid-free paper

For my parents,

Leon and Alice Waldoff

Preface

Intended as a dramaturgical study of Mozart's operas, this book attempts both to illuminate individual works and to offer a substantial treatment of a topic common to them as a group (as well as to operas of Mozart's contemporaries). In many ways, the overall design of the book has been determined by the subject itself. Recognition illuminates certain characters, plots, and themes more than others. The introduction and first three chapters are designed as a sequence; the following chapters are devoted to individual operas and intended as independent but complementary explorations of a central theme.

Because most of the operas discussed here are well known and readily available in a variety of editions, I have provided musical examples only where the discussion seems most to require them. The examples are taken from the Bärenreiter vocal scores, which are based on the Urtext of the *Neue Mozart Ausgabe*, with the exception of those examples in chapter 4 that are taken from the facsimile edition of Niccolò Piccinni's *La buona figliuola* in the Garland series. All have been newly (and expertly) set by Bill Holab of Bill Holab Music.

Passages quoted from the librettos of Mozart's operas are presented in the original language alongside translations designed to be as literal as possible. The sources for these passages are the facsimile editions of the original librettos included in *The Librettos of Mozart's Operas*, edited by Ernest Warburton, with the exception of *La finta giardiniera*, for which I have consulted both the facsimile edition of the Roman libretto of 1774 (included in volume 6 of the same series), upon which Mozart based his opera, and the edition of the opera edited by Rudolph Angermüller and Dietrich Berke in the *Neue Mozart Ausgabe*. Obvious errors of spelling and punctuation in the original librettos have been silently corrected in consultation with the *Neue Mozart Ausgabe*. The translations are mine in some cases and are adapted in others with varying degrees of emendation from the following sources: Gery Bramall's translation of *La finta giardiniera* included in the jacket notes to the Nikolaus Harnoncourt recording (Teldec 9031–72309–2, 1992); and Lionel Salter's translations of

Così fan tutte and *La clemenza di Tito* included in the jacket notes to the John Eliot Gardiner recordings of these operas (Deutsche Grammophon 437 829–2, 1993, and 431 806–2, 1991, respectively).

For discussions of passages from Mozart's letters and documents, I have quoted from the standard editions in English translation: the third edition of *The Letters of Mozart and His Family*, translated by Emily Anderson, and Otto Erich Deutsch's *Mozart: A Documentary Biography*, translated by Eric Blom, Peter Branscombe, and Jeremy Noble. I have, however, occasionally included words and phrases in the original German and/or altered these translations slightly (where indicated) in consultation with *Mozart: Briefe und Aufzeichnungen, Gesamtausgabe* and *Mozart: Die Dokumente seines Lebens*.

I gratefully acknowledge permission granted by Oxford University Press and Cambridge University Press to reproduce three previously published essays here in slightly revised form: chapter 1, which originally appeared as "The Music of Recognition: Operatic Enlightenment in 'The Magic Flute'" in *Music & Letters* 75 (1994); chapter 3, which originated as my principal contribution (sections 1 and 2) to an article jointly authored with James Webster, "Operatic Plotting in *Le nozze di Figaro*," in *Wolfgang Amadè Mozart: Essays on His Life and Music*, edited by Stanley Sadie; and chapter 5, which appeared as "Don Giovanni: Recognition Denied" in *Opera Buffa in Mozart's Vienna*, edited by Mary Hunter and James Webster.

Acknowledgments

The literature on Mozart's operas and their surrounding culture is vast and has
·wn considerably and to my great benefit while I have worked on this book. Al-
·h I have indicated my indebtedness to many authors throughout the book, es-
·n the footnotes, I would like to express special gratitude here to the authors
·ings have influenced me the most: Wye Jamison Allanbrook, Thomas
·e Alan Brown, Daniel Heartz, Mary Hunter, John Platoff, John Rice,
·nd James Webster. I would also like to express my gratitude to Ter-
·magisterial book on recognition inspired this study. Although I
·his book before I had the opportunity to meet him, Terence
· careful and thoughtful readers. His suggestions have im-
·tless ways.
·d friends on whose advice and support I have relied,
·m Webster. It's been many years since I first brought
·ffice hours, but Jim has been an unfailing sup-
·: his comments and suggestions at virtually
·n invaluable. John Platoff read the manu-
·provided criticism and comments that
·a read and reread parts of the manu-
·uggestions. I am grateful to her for
·sistance with and careful review
·support. Karl-Heinz Schoeps
·n and made many valuable
·a special word of thanks,
·ect; his contributions
·tation.
·ered much-needed
·ry Hunter, Kay Knittel,
·ciated encouragement and
·ne other end of the phone when

s;
eir
and
enso,
Calde-
hy, and
on the de-
Robinson,
hlin.
to whom this
velopment and
l. The benefit of
be found on every
ce and has been a
cient words may be
y father and mother,

I needed him. I feel a debt of long standing to several individuals who contributed to the development of these ideas in various ways at an earlier stage: Sarah Adams, Jim Cassaro, Kathryn L. Shanks Libin, Don Randel, David Rosen, and John Winemiller. I am grateful to Tim Carter and Maynard Solomon for their responses long ago to the essay that became chapter 1. I am also grateful to two colleagues who presented me with opportunities that transformed this book: W. Dean Sutcliffe, whose invitation to contribute an essay to his *Haydn Studies* first led me to research opera in a culture of sensibility, and Tony Kaufman, whose invitation to present a paper to the Johnson Society of the Central region (at the University of Illinois at Urbana in 1999) first spurred me to read Mozart "for the sentiment."

Four professors from my years at Amherst College contributed to this project in ways they could not have anticipated: the late Carol Kay, who introduced me to sentimental literature; David Grayson, who introduced me to musicology; the late Henry Mishkin, who gave me my first opportunities to write about Mozart; and William Pritchard, who encouraged me to pursue literature and music first in my honors thesis and then in graduate school. I would also like to say a word of thanks to four friends whose support of this project has taken a less tangible form—Christopher Barber, Osvaldo Golijov, Shirish Korde, and Margaret Webster.

I am grateful to the College of the Holy Cross for a sabbatical leave and research support that were essential to the completion of this book. Alan Karass, our Music Librarian, ever resourceful, has been a wonderful help. Jacky Anderson, our administrative assistant in the Music Department, and Julia Severens, our assistant in the Music Library, deserve thanks for their help with many details over the years. Maria Purciello, who spent a year with us as a lecturer, generously offered assistance whe[n] I needed it. It is with real pleasure that I also extend a word of thanks to my studen[ts;] many of them are fine musicians and a small number are gifted musicologists. Th[eir] questions and requests and enthusiasms have challenged me as both a teache[r and] a scholar. It would be impossible to name them all, but, in addition to Dan DiC[ ] Mark Ferraguto, and Maria Purciello (mentioned above), Marisa Biaggi, Yves[ ] rone, Bethany Collier, Vanessa Kabash, Meredith Lavendar, Evan MacCar[ ] Julia Madden deserve mention here.

I am grateful to everyone at Oxford University Press who has worked[on the de]velopment and production of this book, but especially to my editor Kim[ ] assistant editor Norm Hirschy, and my production editor Christine D[ ]

I do not know how to begin to describe the debt I owe my parents[, to whom this] book is dedicated. My father has read this book at every stage of its de[velopment and] has helped me with countless tasks related to it, both great and sma[ll] his many thoughtful recommendations and editorial comments can[ ] page. My mother, too, has read this book carefully more than o[nce and has been a] constant source of support and encouragement. However insuff[icient] ̣o express such a debt, I would like to conclude by thanking m[ ] ̣ inspired my love of literature and music, respectively.

I needed him. I feel a debt of long standing to several individuals who contributed to the development of these ideas in various ways at an earlier stage: Sarah Adams, Jim Cassaro, Kathryn L. Shanks Libin, Don Randel, David Rosen, and John Winemiller. I am grateful to Tim Carter and Maynard Solomon for their responses long ago to the essay that became chapter 1. I am also grateful to two colleagues who presented me with opportunities that transformed this book: W. Dean Sutcliffe, whose invitation to contribute an essay to his *Haydn Studies* first led me to research opera in a culture of sensibility, and Tony Kaufman, whose invitation to present a paper to the Johnson Society of the Central region (at the University of Illinois at Urbana in 1999) first spurred me to read Mozart "for the sentiment."

Four professors from my years at Amherst College contributed to this project in ways they could not have anticipated: the late Carol Kay, who introduced me to sentimental literature; David Grayson, who introduced me to musicology; the late Henry Mishkin, who gave me my first opportunities to write about Mozart; and William Pritchard, who encouraged me to pursue literature and music first in my honors thesis and then in graduate school. I would also like to say a word of thanks to four friends whose support of this project has taken a less tangible form—Christopher Barber, Osvaldo Golijov, Shirish Korde, and Margaret Webster.

I am grateful to the College of the Holy Cross for a sabbatical leave and research support that were essential to the completion of this book. Alan Karass, our Music Librarian, ever resourceful, has been a wonderful help. Jacky Anderson, our administrative assistant in the Music Department, and Julia Severens, our assistant in the Music Library, deserve thanks for their help with many details over the years. Maria Purciello, who spent a year with us as a lecturer, generously offered assistance when I needed it. It is with real pleasure that I also extend a word of thanks to my students; many of them are fine musicians and a small number are gifted musicologists. Their questions and requests and enthusiasms have challenged me as both a teacher and a scholar. It would be impossible to name them all, but, in addition to Dan DiCenso, Mark Ferraguto, and Maria Purciello (mentioned above), Marisa Biaggi, Yves Calderone, Bethany Collier, Vanessa Kabash, Meredith Lavendar, Evan MacCarthy, and Julia Madden deserve mention here.

I am grateful to everyone at Oxford University Press who has worked on the development and production of this book, but especially to my editor Kim Robinson, assistant editor Norm Hirschy, and my production editor Christine Dahlin.

I do not know how to begin to describe the debt I owe my parents, to whom this book is dedicated. My father has read this book at every stage of its development and has helped me with countless tasks related to it, both great and small. The benefit of his many thoughtful recommendations and editorial comments can be found on every page. My mother, too, has read this book carefully more than once and has been a constant source of support and encouragement. However insufficient words may be to express such a debt, I would like to conclude by thanking my father and mother, who inspired my love of literature and music, respectively.

Acknowledgments

The literature on Mozart's operas and their surrounding culture is vast and has grown considerably and to my great benefit while I have worked on this book. Although I have indicated my indebtedness to many authors throughout the book, especially in the footnotes, I would like to express special gratitude here to the authors whose writings have influenced me the most: Wye Jamison Allanbrook, Thomas Bauman, Bruce Alan Brown, Daniel Heartz, Mary Hunter, John Platoff, John Rice, Julian Rushton, and James Webster. I would also like to express my gratitude to Terence Cave, whose magisterial book on recognition inspired this study. Although I had drafted much of this book before I had the opportunity to meet him, Terence has been one of its most careful and thoughtful readers. His suggestions have improved this volume in countless ways.

Of the many colleagues and friends on whose advice and support I have relied, none has contributed more than Jim Webster. It's been many years since I first brought a copy of Aristotle's *Poetics* to his office hours, but Jim has been an unfailing supporter of this project since that time; his comments and suggestions at virtually every stage of its development have been invaluable. John Platoff read the manuscript in its entirety at a crucial stage and provided criticism and comments that proved extremely helpful. Alessandra Campana read and reread parts of the manuscript as it developed and made many valuable suggestions. I am grateful to her for much stimulating discussion about opera, for her assistance with and careful review of all translations from Italian, and for her unflagging support. Karl-Heinz Schoeps graciously agreed to review all translations from German and made many valuable recommendations. Mark Ferraguto, to whom I want to say a special word of thanks, assisted me in numerous ways during the last year of this project; his contributions have improved the book in matters of content, form, and presentation.

I owe a nearly equal debt of gratitude to several others who offered much-needed assistance and advice at crucial moments: Dan DiCenso, Mary Hunter, Kay Knittel, and Denise Schaeffer. Neal Zaslaw offered much-appreciated encouragement and support as this book took shape and was always at the other end of the phone when

Contents

RECOGNITION IN MOZART'S OPERAS

Introduction

This book explores the ways in which the central themes of Mozart's operas—themes cherished by late eighteenth-century culture such as clemency, constancy, forgiveness, and reconciliation—depend for their dramatization on the same element of plot, recognition. Recognition—or *anagnôrisis*, the term we have inherited from Aristotle's *Poetics*—marks the shift from ignorance to knowledge and involves the protagonist (and the audience) in a powerful reversal of former understanding. It is recognition that holds the key to Sandrina's identity in *La finta giardiniera*, to the contradiction inherent in the King's vow in *Idomeneo*, to the Count's unexpected contrition in *Le nozze di Figaro*, to Fiordiligi's conflicted fidelity in *Così fan tutte*, to Tamino's enlightenment quest in *Die Zauberflöte*. Whether the discovery concerns identity, purpose, or feeling, recognition serves as a vehicle for the thematization of knowledge. Many of these operas turn explicitly on themes of knowledge and discovery, themes that possess a special resonance in an age that named itself the Enlightenment. The ascendance of light in the act 2 finale of *Zauberflöte* is perhaps the most obvious example of how the experience of knowledge may be spectacularly brought to life on the stage, but nearly every contemporary opera ends with some invocation of Enlightenment teachings—whether dramatized primarily in domestic and private terms (as in *Figaro*), in the context of the culture of sensibility (as in *Giardiniera* and *Così*), or with public rhetoric and spectacle (as in *Idomeneo*, *Zauberflöte*, and *La clemenza di Tito*). The conclusions of these operas, whether buffa or seria, whether Italian or German, culminate in a moral, philosophical, or other "truth" that recognition brings, not merely for an individual protagonist or group of characters but for the whole stage and the larger world it represents.

Recognition scenes, of course, are not peculiar to Mozart. They have appeared in opera since its beginnings, and with such regularity that they may be taken as a standard feature of the form—from the personally shattering moment in Monteverdi's *Orfeo* when the hero discovers his mortality to the apocalyptic moment in Wagner's *Ring* when Wotan first imagines and longs for his. As in spoken theater, recognition marks the moments in which major themes and ideas take definitive shape and brings the action to its eventual climax and conclusion. It is not at all surprising, therefore, that opera, which has such rich means of creating and varying voice in drama, would have its own ways of distinguishing these important moments. Opera's complex dynamic of action, text, and music possesses a special potential for realizing dramatic events, and recognition scenes are moments in which that potential is most fully realized.

The special quality of recognition as a vehicle for the gaining of knowledge accounts in large measure for the extent and force of its presence in Mozart's operas, as it does, in fact, in much late eighteenth-century literature, philosophy, and art. As a result, critical thinking about recognition opens up a new way of exploring an important and complex question: the extent to which enlightenment (in several senses of the term) underlies Mozart's operas. Although the diverse movements and ideologies of this period can hardly be thought to share the rubric "Enlightenment" unproblematically, it is clear that the concept of "enlightenment" has particularly rich associations for dramatic representation in this period. It serves as a philosophical and cultural backdrop to the action and at the same time offers a metaphor for the gaining of knowledge that may be vividly represented on the stage. A focus on recognition also provides a new perspective on many other issues central to understanding these works and prominent in current critical conversations about the operas of Mozart and his contemporaries. Among the most important of these are the role of sensibility in his works; the representation of women and of attitudes toward them; the status of the plot and its musical mechanisms in late eighteenth-century opera; and the problem(s) of Mozart's conventional endings and their troubled reception from his day to ours.

Recognition: "From Ignorance to Knowledge"

As a dramatic device, recognition has a rich and complex history in both literature and literary studies. In over four hundred years of writing about opera, by contrast, and despite considerable deliberation over the nature of operatic drama, recognition scenes have been almost entirely neglected. Literary theory thus provides an invaluable framework for thinking about recognition in opera. It seems necessary, therefore, before turning to the subject of recognition in Mozart's operas, to offer a brief consideration of both classical and contemporary views on the subject. I shall begin with Aristotle, whose *Poetics* offers the first articulation of the concept and the one to which all later considerations of the topic are indebted:

> Recognition [*anagnôrisis*], as the very name shows, is a change from ignorance
> to knowledge, bringing the characters into either a close bond, or enmity,
> with one another, and concerning matters which bear on their prosperity or
> affliction. The finest recognition occurs in direct conjunction with reversal

[*peripeteia*]—as with the one in the *Oedipus*. There are, of course, other kinds of recognition, for recognition can relate to inanimate or fortuitous objects, or reveal that someone has, or has not, committed a deed. But the type I have mentioned is the one which is most integral to the plot-structure and its action: for such a combination of recognition and reversal will produce pity or fear (and it is events of this kind that tragedy, on our definition, is a mimesis of), since both affliction and prosperity will hinge on such circumstances.[1]

Reversal, or *peripeteia,* is brought about by "a complete swing in the direction of the action," one that produces the opposite effect of what was intended.[2] In the *Poetics*, recognition and reversal are two of the three elements of plot (the third is suffering, or *pathos*) and are most frequently discussed in the context of what Aristotle calls "complex" plots.[3] The finest recognition, according to Aristotle, is one that comes in the course of a complex action at the same moment as a peripeteia and is brought about by the events themselves. This last point is crucial, as we can see by Aristotle's choice of Sophocles' *Oedipus* as his paradigmatic example. The recognition in the play is brought about by the events of the plot and is accompanied by a peripeteia. Oedipus sought to avoid fulfilling the prophecy of the oracle, but in the end his actions are revealed, in a powerful recognition scene, to have brought about the very thing he feared. We need not concern ourselves at this point with Aristotle's elaborate typology and ranking of recognitions, except to observe his still influential view that the finest type is that brought about by the events of the plot.[4]

Aristotle is particular in stating that peripeteia is the shift in one continuous action. In the example he discusses most fully, *Oedipus*, this shift is the single climax of the drama. His definition is biased in favor of plots that move toward the revelation of hidden or unknown identity, and in which the discovery of identity becomes a moment of both recognition and reversal, as when Oedipus discovers who he is. It is also generally the case, as in *Oedipus*, that such a reversal occurs near the end, bringing about a recognition after which everything will be significantly and forever changed. There may, however, be more recognitions than one in a single plot, and this is as true for detective fiction or opera as for Greek tragedy. The ultimate recognition will thus turn out to be the result of shifts, discoveries, and/or small or even partial moments of awareness that occurred earlier in the plot. In this

1. Aristotle, *Poetics*, trans. Halliwell (11), 43. See also Halliwell's discussion of this passage, 116–20. All quotations of Aristotle's *Poetics*, unless otherwise indicated, are from this translation and identified by chapter and page.

2. *Poetics* (11), 42. See also Else's translation, where the definition is given as "a shift of what is being undertaken to the opposite" (35).

3. Aristotle defines the "complex" action as "one whose transformation involves recognition or reversal, or both" (*Poetics* [10], 42). For his definition of *pathos* and the distinction between "simple" and "complex" plots, see *Poetics* (11), 43, and (10), 42, respectively.

4. Aristotle's five types of recognition are enumerated in *Poetics* (16), 48–49; for a discussion of these, see chapter 2.

respect, reversal, contrast, discovery, and change of action or fortune are the stuff of which all plots are made. The climactic recognition at the end cannot be thought to stand alone. It satisfies to the degree that it does precisely because it mirrors and has grown out of a series of smaller discoveries.

Recognition holds two further implications for the stories in which it plays a part, each of which involves a double sense of the term itself. The first is concerned with what recognition is. Where recognition or knowledge itself is the subject of a story (which is often the case, as in *Zauberflöte*), it is developed in two ways, as I have already suggested: as a function of the plot and as a central theme. This double sense is what Terence Cave has called the "double character of recognition." "Recognition," he explains, "as both formal device and vehicle for themes of knowledge allows one the latitude to move freely between formal poetics and interpretation."[5] This double character implies that the act of recognition itself mediates the move from issues of form to those of content and back again.

The second implication entails an important and particular double meaning contained within the term itself: recognition is both new awareness and re-cognition. To recognize is to re-cognize, that is, to know again, but to do so in a way that involves new understanding. It implies the recovery of something already known. Knowledge is therefore inherent in recognition; it lies concealed, deep within memory, waiting to be brought to the surface. To the extent that recognitions depend on memory, even though memory recovered with new understanding, they involve a repetition of recollected events and thoughts. Hence recognition always involves narrative. This point cannot be overemphasized: recognition always comes as part of a story. Brought about by one narrative, recognition reaches back to another narrative (or episode) for its explanation, which, when it comes, conflates past and present in a powerful moment of new awareness. The protagonist of a drama or fiction (or the individual who recounts the story of his or her life) encounters something new that contains within it some recollection, some trace of the past.[6] The crucial element here is repetition: a word, a story, a sound, or an event that triggers recognition. This repetition brings to mind some former event that is at least in part repeated (if only by reference) as it is remembered, and is now understood with new awareness.

Recognition therefore implies both the gaining and the regaining of knowledge. Its paradoxical nature is complicated and enriched by the overlay of connotation and critical history, as well as of literal and figurative meanings. Ambiguity and complexity lie at the heart of it. The challenge for opera studies is to find a way to understand recognition in terms appropriate—perhaps even exclusive—to opera, where recognition is almost always realized in musical terms. In operas of different periods, genres, and traditions, however, recognition scenes do not obey any specific set

---

5. Cave, *Recognitions*, 4. I am especially indebted to this book for my understanding of the topic.
6. This is also the situation of the analysand. Two works of Freud's of special interest in this connection—that is, the return of the repressed and repetition—are "The Uncanny" and *Beyond the Pleasure Principle.*

of musical patterns or rules; they appear in various keys, tempos, or styles, and in a wide variety of recitative, aria, ensemble, and other forms. Still, recognition, in opera as in other genres, is central to understanding themes, characters, plot complications, dénouements, and conclusions. Critical application of the idea to individual works, as even Aristotle demonstrates, is riddled with complications, but it should be not only possible but analytically productive to adapt this concept from the world of literature to that of musical drama, even though it will first have to be rethought and recontextualized for the purpose. In this book, I have attempted just such an adaptation, and one in which a virtue may be made of the attendant complications.

Recognition as a New Perspective

In opera as in literature, recognition—if mentioned at all—has generally been regarded as a jaded convention. The issue of plot, essential to any discussion of recognition, has also been marginalized, particularly in studies of Mozart's operas, and in two notable ways: the plots of operas have, as a matter of course, been passed over as too "obvious" to warrant serious attention, but they have also frequently been disparaged. Indeed, many operas are as notorious for their purportedly absurd plots as renowned for their musical expression. Most important, even though opera is properly understood as both a literary and a musical kind of drama (one that involves text, music, and action), it has often been viewed primarily as a musical genre. As a result, dramatic issues in opera have tended to be defined in terms of musical phenomena—aria types, musical textures, ensemble and finale forms, tonal planning, and musico-dramatic events such as recurring themes—rather than in terms of the elements essential to understanding opera as drama, such as plot types, conventions of ending, character development, and, of course, recognitions and the reversals they bring.

Joseph Kerman summed up this problem in his seminal 1956 study, *Opera as Drama*, when he identified two prevailing views that, perhaps more than any others, have inhibited the study of opera: "the one held by musicians, that opera is a low form of music, and the one apparently held by everybody else, that opera is a low form of drama."[7] At the same time, it is a long-held and understandable belief of opera critics that whatever is truly important and persuasive in opera must happen in the music. We trust the music first and last, and if something of great consequence transpires in opera but remains *unconfirmed* by the music, we tend to consider it suspect. The unfortunate corollary of this belief, however, has been a privileging of the musical perspective, at times to the exclusion of other aspects of operatic drama. To view opera *as* drama, therefore, requires more than just an approach that joins musical and literary perspectives; it requires an approach in which the musical dimension of opera is neither overestimated nor underestimated. A focus on recognition

---

7. Kerman, *Opera as Drama*, 16.

offers a new perspective on some of the particular difficulties that inhere in the study of opera.

To the extent it can be gleaned from the writings of contemporary librettists and composers, the history of opera in this period reads as a constant struggle to reconcile the demands of musical form on the one hand, and those of dramatic action on the other. Chafing in his *Memoirs* that the "hollow devices" of opera buffa may reflect badly on the poet, for example, Mozart's best-known librettist, Lorenzo da Ponte, decries the conventional structure of the opera buffa finale, which requires the inclusion of a singing part for every member of the cast, "and if the plot of the drama does not permit, the poet must find a way to make it permit, in the face of reason, good sense, Aristotle, and all the powers of heaven or earth; and if then the *finale* happens to go badly, so much the worse for him!"[8] In the dedication to *Alceste,* Gluck offers sharp criticism of the operatic conventions of his day and claims that in this work he has "sought to abolish all the abuses against which good sense and reason have long cried out in vain."[9] Like librettists and composers of Mozart's day, critics and commentators of later eras have struggled to resolve the conflict between musical form and dramatic content, and much critical thinking about Mozart's operas can be characterized by some of the problems that have arisen as a result.

Let me summarize briefly just five of these problems. First, analysis in the operatic context is, by definition, multivalent and multidisciplinary. It involves an approach that is both musical and literary, as Kerman has suggested, but it also requires something more. Wagner offered his view of this analytical challenge long ago when he insisted that musical drama ought to comprise "acts of music made visible" ("ersichtlich gewordene Taten der Musik").[10] But in his theory of the *Gesamtkunstwerk* he assumed a "unity" of text, music, and action—a "unity" in which elements of musical construction are privileged—that came to dominate opera studies, including the field of Mozart's operas. As a concept and an analytical goal, unity has become increasingly suspect in today's critical climate. Opera is a fundamentally intertextual medium; its component parts do not always work together and may often be shown to contradict one another. Some of the most interesting recent work in the field of Mozart's operas (and in opera studies in general) is characterized by thinking about this issue.

Second, as performative art, opera is a genre for which there is neither "text" nor "score" in the ordinary sense. And while this is true for opera in general, it is particularly important for late eighteenth-century opera. The surviving sources are now widely regarded as woefully inadequate reflections of what may have happened on any particular stage on any given evening. The first printed libretto and the autograph score, for example, often contradict one another. In Mary Hunter's words,

---

8. Da Ponte, *Memoirs,* 59–60.

9. Gluck, "Dedication to *Alceste,*" in Strunk, ed., *Source Readings in Music History,* 933.

10. Wagner, "Über die Benennung 'Musikdrama,'" 306.

"The notion of 'the work' then becomes not the final thoughts of a single creator, or even the final thoughts of two 'authors' (composer and librettist), but rather an ongoing collaboration between those authors and what might otherwise be thought to be its 'context'—the performers, set designers, censors, and other figures vital to establishing what played on any given evening."[11] In some cases, famously in that of the Viennese run of *Don Giovanni*, we cannot even be certain how the opera ends. Attempts to fix or standardize a version of the "work" that can be studied have motivated scholars to expand the field of source studies beyond the making of critical editions to include the pursuit of manuscript copies, early editions, performing parts, librettos, prompt books, letters, and theatrical records. This work is invaluable, but it is not centered on dramatic questions.

Third, in part because of the difficulty of isolating the object of study, the operatic "work," the consideration of any given operatic context or culture is enormously complex. As Lorenzo Bianconi has shown in his discussion of Venetian opera in the seventeenth century, opera needs to be understood as both an art form (a distinct genre with its own conventions and habits) and an "institution" (a theatrical company associated with a particular city and building, devoted to the business of pleasing consumers and making a profit).[12] It has become commonplace in the last twenty years to speak of librettists, directors, designers, and singers as a composer's collaborators, and to draw on the social, economic, and ideological circumstances of any given opera, as well as on the history of the theater for which it was written, including its personnel, repertoire, and audience. This kind of activity, which has opened the field to fascinating questions about reception history and genre, has, not surprisingly, divided opera studies into culturally and historically defined subareas: public opera in seventeenth-century Venice, opera buffa in Mozart's Vienna, French grand opera, Verdi studies, Wagner studies, and so on. Like source studies, this perspective, however, has understandably not favored larger questions of operatic drama.

Fourth, the dominant analytical tradition in studies of Mozart's operas until very recently has been grounded in a bias against the libretto. For example, although nearly everyone acknowledges that *Zauberflöte* contains great music, many have considered it highly implausible, second-rate drama. Emanuel Schikaneder's libretto is regarded, in the oft-cited words of Edward Dent, as "one of the most absurd specimens of that form of literature in which absurdity is regarded as a matter of course."[13] Mozart's sublime music, it is believed, must overcome, transform, even transcend its libretto. This long-standing view of the libretto as a low form of literature has led to a privileging of matters of exclusively musical construction over dramaturgical concerns that inhere in the libretto and its plot. But these "pure-music"

11. Hunter, *Culture of Opera Buffa*, 16.
12. Bianconi, *Music in the Seventeenth Century*, 161–70.
13. Dent, *Mozart's Operas*, 218.

approaches—for that is what they are—assume at the very least a subordination of text to music, if not an outright separation of music from both its text and context. No method could be more inappropriate for opera.

Fifth, due in large part to this dismissive stance toward the libretto, Mozart's operatic music has often been studied not merely from a predominantly musical but from a particularly instrumental perspective. This approach is directly descended from the Romantics' exaltation of instrumental music as "absolute" music—something, as Carl Dahlhaus reminds us, that may be regarded as "art-religion."[14] According to this view, instrumental music, which, in E. T. A. Hoffmann's famous formulation, "scorns all assistance from and combination with other art," reigns as the *non plus ultra* of musical drama.[15] Ironically, this metaphoric notion of "drama" borrowed from instrumental models came to dominate thinking about Mozart's operas, at times even to replace the literal sense of drama intrinsic to opera as a theatrical medium. Opera's overt "drama" was thus marginalized and subverted, and this tendency has been reinforced by the fact that the models for appreciating and analyzing Mozart's instrumental music were in place long ago. For example, the privileging of ensembles over arias, which has long characterized the literature, surely has its origins in the ease with which sonata form—or at least a "sonata principle"—may be shown to underlie the formal structure of many ensembles.[16] And while it must be said that a focus on instrumental models has revealed much about the construction of individual numbers and need not necessarily be understood as excluding or overriding considerations of text or plot, it has more often than not done just that. Instrumental models have frequently been used to "free" operatic music from what were thought of as the encumbrances of plot, character, and staging, and, at the same time, to lift it above the controversies surrounding them. Musical drama was thus transmuted into dramatic music—a practice that undoubtedly has its origins in Wagner's attempts in writing to distinguish the opera of his day from his music dramas.

Figaro's "Scar" as the "Signature of a Fiction"

The neglect of recognition, then, may be understood as part and parcel of the opera-as-drama problem. Indeed, the value of recognition as a new perspective for the study of Mozart's operas lies precisely in its status as a dramatic rather than a musical approach. At the same time, it must be acknowledged that recognition scenes are not only moments of resolution and completion; they are also problem moments,

14. See Dahlhaus, *Idea of Absolute Music.*

15. Hoffmann, "Review of the Fifth Symphony," 151.

16. Examples of such "sonata form" analyses of operatic numbers are too numerous to mention. The term "sonata principle" originates in Cone, *Musical Form and Musical Performance,* 76–77. A discussion of it in relation to Mozart's operas appears in Carter, *W. A. Mozart: "Le nozze di Figaro,"* 89–90. On the privileging of ensembles, see Webster, "Analysis of Mozart's Arias," especially 101–5; and Hunter, *Culture of Opera Buffa,* 156–57.

moments that strain belief and call attention to the contrivance and quality of artifice that inhere in fictional plots. "The recognition scene," as Cave has observed, "is, as it were, the mark or signature of a fiction, so that even if something like it occurs in fact, it still sounds like fiction and will probably be retold as such."[17] Take, for example, a scene from *Figaro* that Mozart's friend Michael Kelly (the tenor who created the roles of Basilio and Don Curzio in the first production) tells us was the composer's favorite: the scene in act 3 in which the discovery of a spatula-shaped birthmark on Figaro's arm reveals him to be the long-lost son of his archenemies Marcellina and Bartolo.[18] This recognition scene marks a crucial reversal in the plot. It releases Figaro from the contract that binds him to either repay the money he owes Marcellina or marry her, for, as the lawyer Don Curzio is the first to observe, Figaro cannot marry his own mother. It transforms Marcellina and Bartolo into doting parents who are now glad to forgive their newly recovered son his outstanding debt and to embrace Susanna as a daughter. Finally, to the Count's dismay, it removes the last obstacle in the way of Figaro's marriage to Susanna. It is difficult to imagine a coincidence more fortuitous or more unlikely. It is as if this recognition scene was designed to call attention to the construction of the plot and the implausibility of its fiction, to the fact of its participation in a comedy. And it does so by making deliberate sport of the conventions of recognition.

Following the Beaumarchais play upon which the libretto is based, this scene combines aspects of two well-known recognition scenes from the Classical period— scenes treated as paradigmatic in the *Poetics*—into one implausible scenario. The spatula-shaped birthmark that triggers the discovery is, of course, a comic version of Odysseus's "scar," the mark by which his old nurse recognizes him on his return to Ithaca. Thus when Bartolo tells Figaro that Marcellina is his mother, Figaro counters, "Balia?" (My nurse?), as if to point out that in a proper recreation of this scene the woman to identify his scar would be his nurse, not his mother. At the same time, the comic discovery of identity by means of this "scar," fortunately indeed for Figaro, occurs in time to prevent him from marrying his mother and enduring the tragic recognition of Oedipus.[19] Here, fused by an extraordinary contrivance of the poet (or poets), are the two recognition scenes that Aristotle offers as examples of the weakest and the finest of his five types: that of Odysseus, which is brought about by means of a "token" and has been viewed since as the hallmark of the contrived or

17. Cave, *Recognitions*, 4.

18. Michael Kelly, *Reminiscences*, 260. Kelly goes on to say that Mozart asked him to refrain from stuttering in the sextet (as Kelly created him, Don Curzio stuttered in other scenes) because it would spoil the music.

19. Figaro himself acknowledges the oedipal situation in Beaumarchais's play, exclaiming shortly after the revelation is made to him: "After all the times I've refrained from breaking this gentleman's neck because of his cursed hundred crowns—he now turns out to be my father! However, since Heaven has prevented me from committing a crime, accept my apologies, Father. And you, Mother, embrace me—as maternally as you can." Beaumarchais, *The Barber of Seville and the Marriage of Figaro*, 177. See, among others, D. W. Howarth, "The Recognition-Scene in 'Le Mariage de Figaro.'"

conventional recognition, and that of Oedipus, which is brought about by the events themselves. Such a moment as this one in *Figaro* may be enjoyed as much for its ingenious construction as for the happy reconciliation it makes possible on stage. Mozart sets the moment of discovery as recitative; the emotional reconciliation it makes possible immediately unfolds in the opening lines of the sextet "Riconosci in questo amplesso" as Figaro embraces his newly discovered family. When Susanna enters during the sextet to discover Figaro in Marcellina's arms, confusion, discovery, and reconciliation are immediately replayed to create a second recognition scene for her.

It would be difficult to point to more convincing evidence that Aristotle's *Poetics* and its paradigms were alive and well in the world of Mozart's theater or that the multiple authors of the *Figaro* story were aware of the significance (and origin) of recognition scenes. At the same time, this complex and critically self-reflective recognition illustrates how recognition can problematize the very sense of closure it attempts to bring about. Here is Cave:

> Recognition scenes in literary works are by their nature "problem" moments rather than moments of satisfaction and completion. Anagnorisis seems at first sight to be the paradigm of narrative satisfaction: it answers questions, restores identity and symmetry, and makes a whole hidden structure of relations intelligible. Yet the satisfaction is also somehow excessive, the reassurance too easy; the structure is visibly prone to collapse.[20]

The discovery of Figaro's lineage neatly resolves a number of plot difficulties and reveals a "whole hidden structure of relations" vital to the outcome of the opera, but the reconciliation seems, to borrow Cave's attractive phrase, like "the mark or signature of a fiction," too good to be true. In the Beaumarchais play, Figaro, reflecting on the events of the day in act 5, even betrays a sense of disbelief at the extraordinary way in which he escapes Oedipus's fate: "I'm on the point of falling into an abyss and marrying my own mother when, lo and behold, my parents turn up one after the other! (*He rises.*) Debate and discussion. It's you, it's him, it's me, it's thee, no, it isn't any of us, no, who is it then? (*Falls into his seat again.*) Oh! Fantastic series of events!"[21] Mozart allows his setting to reflect the extraordinary unlikelihood of these events in several ways. First, at the moment of recognition in the recitative, when Marcellina exclaims, "È desso" (It is he), Figaro replies, "È ver, son io" (Indeed, it is I) over a sustained dominant seventh sonority. But the significance of his statement is precisely that he does not yet realize who he is, something Da Ponte and Mozart emphasize when Don Curzio, the Count, and Bartolo all exclaim in rapid succession "Chi?" "Chi?" "Chi?" (Who?). The suspense is relieved when the harmony

20. Cave, *Recognitions,* 489.
21. Beaumarchais, *The Barber of Seville and the Marriage of Figaro,* 202.

resolves to G minor and Marcellina provides Figaro with the answer, "Raffaello." But Figaro responds to this news with pointed disbelief, first by suggesting that she was his nurse and then by exclaiming, "Cosa sento!" (What do I hear!).

When in the sextet Marcellina identifies herself to Susanna as Figaro's mother, Mozart again emphasizes the implausibility of this turn of events and in an even more striking manner. Susanna's query, "Sua madre?" (His mother?) to which all reply "Sua madre!" is transformed into an amusing little drama in its own right. Susanna responds to Marcellina's extraordinary statement with complete incredulity, addressing her question, "Sua madre?" to each character in turn. When she finally asks the question of Figaro, still in disbelief, he assumes the question of Marcellina's identity is settled and presents his father to her instead, allowing the entire exchange to be replayed on the words "Suo padre." Here is Mozart's rendering of what were originally only six lines of verse in the libretto:

SUSANNA (TO BARTOLO)
Sua madre?   His mother?

BARTOLO
    Sua madre!   His mother!

SUSANNA (TO THE COUNT)
Sua madre?   His mother?

THE COUNT
    Sua madre!   His mother!

SUSANNA (TO DON CURZIO)
Sua madre?   His mother?

DON CURZIO
    Sua madre!   His mother!

SUSANNA (TO MARCELLINA)
Sua madre?   His mother?

MARCELLINA
    Sua madre ...   His mother ...

MARCELLINA, THE COUNT, DON CURZIO, BARTOLO
Sua madre, sua madre!   His mother, his mother!

SUSANNA (TO FIGARO)
Tua madre?   Your mother?

FIGARO
E quello è mio padre,   And this is my father,
Che a te lo dirà.   as he will tell you himself.

SUSANNA (TO BARTOLO)
Suo padre?   His father?

BARTOLO
         Suo padre!   His father!

SUSANNA (TO THE COUNT)
Suo padre?   His father?

THE COUNT
         Suo padre!   His father!

SUSANNA (TO DON CURZIO)
Suo padre?   His father?

DON CURZIO
         Suo padre!   His father!

SUSANNA (TO MARCELLINA)
Suo padre?   His father?

MARCELLINA
         Suo padre . . .   His father . . .

MARCELLINA, THE COUNT, DON CURZIO, BARTOLO
Suo padre, suo padre!   His father, his father!

SUSANNA (TO FIGARO)
Tuo padre?   Your father?

FIGARO
E quella è mia madre,   And this is my mother,
Che a te lo dirà.   as she will tell you herself.

As both dramatist and critic, Mozart cleverly composes the resistance to recognition into his sextet. At precisely the moment of greatest musico-dramatic satisfaction (m. 74), the moment when all is revealed to the unsuspecting Susanna, Marcellina moves to embrace her daughter-in-law to be, restoring the tonic and returning to the original melody with which she had embraced Figaro at the ensemble's opening. But Susanna responds to this "recapitulation" (and its implied reconciliation) with understandable mistrust. As her ensuing questions show, satisfaction is indeed "excessive," reassurance both "easy" and dubious.[22]

That recognition scenes are also "problem" moments suggests an additional value of studying their role in Mozart's operas. Often the moments criticized as contrived or poorly constructed in treatments of these operas—the very moments held

22. For a different reading of this scene, see Castelvecchi, "Sentimental and Anti-Sentimental in *Le nozze di Figaro.*"

made manifest by the use of veils. At the end of act 1, the initiates Tamino and Papageno are led off stage with their heads veiled, and from this point forward their actual veiling and unveiling is explicit. The veils—and the darkness they necessarily impose—are an important part of the ritual of the trials. For example, Tamino and Papageno are veiled as they are led on stage for the first test, that of silence; the veils are removed as the test begins, and are replaced when the test is passed and the two are again led off. Sarastro describes Tamino's entrance to the trials as his seeking to tear off the veil of night and to see into the sanctuary of great light ("dieser Jüngling will seinen nächtlichen Schleier von sich reißen, und ins Heiligtum des größten Lichtes blicken").

The central drama turns on the symbolic opposition of light and dark, and the move from darkness to light is the dominant metaphor employed in the opera for the gaining of knowledge. First suggested by Tamino's "O ewige Nacht! Wann wirst du schwinden? / Wann wird das Licht mein Auge finden?" (O eternal night! When will you end? / When will my eyes find the light?), enlightenment (literally and figuratively) becomes the object of Tamino's quest when, in the second act, he seeks membership in the sacred order. The metaphor pervades the language used to develop themes of knowledge. The image of the coming of light (dawn) complements the coming of knowledge as the three boys begin the act 2 finale: "Bald prangt, den Morgen zu verkünden, / Die Sonn' auf goldner Bahn" (Soon, to herald the morning, the sun will shine on its golden path). It also permeates the remarks of the priests, as in the following line from the chorus "O Isis, und Osiris, welche Wonne!" in act 2 (No. 18): "Die düstre Nacht verscheucht der Glanz der Sonne" (The dark night is banished by the brightness of the sun). Other uses of the same metaphor include Papageno's telling outburst in the dialogue before the act 2 quintet No. 12: "He, Lichter her! Lichter her!—Das ist doch wunderlich, so oft einen die Herrn verlassen, so sieht man mit offenen Augen nichts." ("Hey, lights over here! Lights over here! How strange! As soon as these men leave you, you can't see a thing with your eyes open.") When the enlightened leave Papageno, he is figuratively—and in this case literally—in the dark.

The Queen's fear of enlightenment is represented not only by her role as supreme monarch of darkness and by her plotting against Sarastro and his realm but also in her language. She tells Pamina that Tamino will be lost to her, "wenn du nicht, eh' die Sonne die Erde färbt, ihn durch diese unterirdischen Gewölbe zu fliehen beredest.— Der erste Schimmer des Tages entscheidet, ob er ganz dir oder den Eingeweihten gegeben sei" (unless you persuade him to flee through these subterranean vaults before the sun tinges the earth—the first glimmer of day will decide whether he is given to you wholly or to the enlightened ones). The dawn's first light will carry Tamino out of the reach of the Queen's power and, so she imagines, of her daughter's as well. To summarize, the use of language in the libretto develops the quest for enlightenment as a complex idea of light, reason, knowledge, love, and friendship—a quest for everything aligned on the bright side of the symbolic opposition of light and dark.

In addition to being the dominant metaphor within the opera, the theme of enlightenment (as I have already suggested) is played out against an obvious historical and ideological backdrop. The quest for knowledge in *Zauberflöte* is a double quest: for knowledge *of* the self and *for* the self. This view of knowledge often found expression in the age, and had some currency outside the philosopher's study. For example, when the *Berlinische Monatsschrift* posed the question "What is Enlightenment?" no less a figure than Immanuel Kant responded (in company with Gotthold Lessing, Moses Mendelssohn, and many others). Kant's short essay was published by the journal in December 1784 under the title, "Beantwortung der Frage: Was ist Aufklärung?" (In Response to the Question: What Is Enlightenment?). Here Kant presents his own definition for the age. In it he emphasizes that an individual must learn through self-awareness:

> Enlightenment is man's leaving his self-caused immaturity. Immaturity is the incapacity to use one's intelligence without the guidance of another. Such immaturity is self-caused if it is not caused by lack of intelligence, but by lack of determination and courage to use one's intelligence without being guided by another. *Sapere Aude!* Have the courage to use your own intelligence! is therefore the motto of the enlightenment.[4]

Faith is not inherited truth in Kant's philosophy, but something that an individual comes to know through thought and self-development. Similarly, enlightenment is not conferred knowledge; it may only be achieved by those who resolve to seek it. (In this context, it is worth noting Schiller's famous response to Kant's injunction: "Dare to be wise!" ["Erkühne dich, weise zu sein"]).[5]

To what extent Mozart and Schikaneder felt a loyalty to any so-designated Enlightenment ideals, as represented in a manifesto such as Kant's, is difficult, perhaps impossible, to determine. What we know for certain is that the "Enlightenment" question was of contemporaneous concern in Vienna. Johann Pezzl discusses it in his *Skizze von Wien* (1786–1790): "The nonsensical clamourings from all quarters of the German lands during the last decade (more or less) concerning the *word* 'Enlightenment' have almost made the *cause* itself an object of general ridicule. . . . Such infantile babblings must not, however, be allowed to deflect us from honouring and advancing the real Enlightenment."[6] And one would have to go out of one's way to ignore the fact that the central theme of *Zauberflöte* is also the theme of the age. In addition, both Schikaneder and Mozart were Freemasons, and the Masons in late eighteenth-century Vienna espoused many of the philosophical and political ideals also claimed as Enlightenment. Contemporary evidence reveals that from the first

---

4. Kant, "What Is Enlightenment?" 132.
5. See Schiller, *On the Aesthetic Education of Man,* 48–53.
6. Johann Pezzl, "Sketch of Vienna," in Landon, *Mozart and Vienna,* 128. I have amended Landon's translation slightly; see Johann Pezzl, *Skizze von Wien,* 381.

the opera's use of symbol and ritual was connected with Freemasonry. The frontispiece for the original libretto, for example, published by Ignaz Alberti, a fellow Mason and member of Mozart's own lodge, *Zur Neugekrönten Hoffnung*, strongly suggests Masonic connections in its imagery and symbolism.[7] The sacred band of Sarastro and his priests has long been taken to represent a Masonic order. Indeed, several of the men involved in the first performance were known to be Masons, and the Masonic symbolism is overt: the sevenfold sun emblem, the emphasis upon the number three, and particularly the initiation rites including the test of silence and the trials by fire and water.

Nor was this Mozart's first engagement with Masonic ritual in the theater. Tobias Philipp von Gebler's play *Thamos, König in Ägypten,* for which Mozart had earlier composed incidental music for performances in Salzburg, tells the story of a high priest who rules in a temple of the sun and wears a sun emblem. Mozart's music for this Masonic allegory includes the so-called threefold chord, later to become the hallmark gesture of *Zauberflöte,* as well as "priestly" music similar to that in the later opera.[8] Many have suggested that the character of this gesture and of the music of the priests in *Thamos,* both unquestionably Masonic in the context of Gebler's play, reveal the Masonic underpinnings of *Zauberflöte.*[9] Some have even gone so far as to suppose that the opera may be understood as a defense of the Masons, a subtle way of pleading the order's cause in difficult times. But whatever Mozart's and Schikaneder's motives may have been (about which there has been much speculation), no one would deny that *Zauberflöte* reflects several of the major themes and concerns of its age.

Against this background, *Zauberflöte* may be understood as an allegory of enlightenment. The shift to the enlightened state, by definition, implies the gaining of knowledge. Its vehicle is recognition. In terms of its dramaturgy, *Zauberflöte* is based on a "quest" plot, centering on a recognition scene. Tamino's quest for knowledge is a dramatization of the theme of enlightenment, and reaches a climax at moments when he achieves new awareness, particularly in the recitative scene with the priest in the act 1 finale (a scene considered in detail below). When the plot of *Zauberflöte* is considered in the context of its theme of enlightenment, the quest at the heart of it assumes a new significance for understanding the opera as musical drama. Recog-

7. The oft-reproduced frontispiece may be found with a brief discussion in Landon, *1791,* plate 9 and pp. 127–37. Of the many detailed Masonic interpretations of the opera, see especially Nettl, *Mozart and Masonry;* Rosenberg, *Die Zauberflöte;* and Chailley, *Magic Flute.*

8. King, "Melodic Sources and Affinities of *Die Zauberflöte,*" 242 and 249.

9. The presentation of Masonic ritual in both *Thamos* and *Zauberflöte* has also been traced to a French novel by the *abbé* Jean Terrasson, *Sethos* (1731), first translated into German in 1732, and again in 1778. Among the many who have developed the connection are Nettl, *Mozart and Masonry,* 69–80; Rosenberg, *Zauberflöte,* 167–80; and Branscombe, *W. A. Mozart: "Die Zauberflöte,"* 10–20. For an excellent treatment of *Sethos* and the influence of Masonic ritual in the opera, see Koenigsberger, "New Metaphor for Mozart's *The Magic Flute.*"

nition is thus crucial to the opera in two respects: as an aspect of the plot and as a central theme.

Tamino's Recognition: "Wann wird das Licht mein Auge finden?"

I turn now to the crucial recognition scene in *Zauberflöte*, Tamino's great recitative colloquy with the priest. Among others who have focused attention on this scene and suggested its central role in the drama are Rodney Farnsworth, James Webster, and Christoph Wolff.[10] My understanding of this passage, however, differs from theirs in two fundamental respects: first, I provide an analysis of it as a recognition scene; and second, I consider this scene with respect to the opera as a whole, taking recognition as a key to the plot and as a dominant theme of the work.[11]

At the beginning of the finale in act 1, Tamino's quest for Pamina has brought him to Sarastro's realm, specifically to the gates of the three temples of Wisdom, Reason, and Nature. But the priest who greets Tamino will not let him pass, and their conversation leaves Tamino in confusion. "Wann also wird die Decke schwinden?" (When then will the veil be lifted?), he asks finally. "Sobald dich führt der Freundschaft Hand, / Ins Heiligtum zum ew'gen Band" (As soon as the hand of friendship leads you into the holy place to the eternal order), the priest answers in parting, leaving Tamino alone. Now comes the moment of recognition: "O ewige Nacht!" Tamino cries, "Wann wirst du schwinden? / Wann wird das Licht mein Auge finden?" (O eternal night! When will you end? / When will light strike my eyes?).

Tamino has suddenly become aware that his understanding of Pamina's abduction, of the Queen's distress, of Sarastro's true nature—and thus, his understanding of his world and of himself—is false. The night seems eternal because the "truth," the knowledge that he seeks, has been denied him. But his exclamation is an important turning point. He had not questioned the Queen's story, and had believed her to be good and Sarastro evil. Tamino's new awareness is a reversal of his former understanding: it is a moment of recognition. What is more, to paraphrase Aristotle, Tamino's recognition comes as the direct result of the events themselves. In this context, of course, such events may not be understood singly as events of action, text, or music; they must be understood as composite, operatic events.

This scene takes the form of a long and complex accompanied recitative, an unusual occurrence in an eighteenth-century German opera.[12] As recitative, the scene

10. See Farnsworth, "Tamino at the Temple's Portals"; Webster, "To Understand Verdi and Wagner"; and Wolff, "'O ew'ge Nacht!'"

11. As far as I know, the term *recognition* has not been employed in an analysis of the opera, with the single exception of Baker, "'Night into Day.'" But he does not provide a detailed analysis of this or any other scene, and he does not offer any serious consideration of recognition as a topic.

12. For a discussion of the prevalence of dialogue as opposed to recitative in eighteenth-century German opera, see Bauman, *North German Opera*, 9–14; and Bauman, "Benda, the Germans, and Simple Recitative."

Example 1.1.   *Continued*

As this first half of the dialogue proceeds, Tamino challenges the priest. But the priest reveals that Sarastro rules here, even in the Temple of Wisdom. Horrified, Tamino makes to leave, and his gesture is accompanied by a poignant orchestral figure (marked "x" in example 1.2). This gesture is then repeated a second and a third time, before the priest convinces him to remain.

From the midpoint of the dialogue, when Tamino is persuaded to stay, the predominance of sudden *forte* markings and the occasional tremolo for Tamino, and sustained, quiet lines for the priest, are the only norms. Furious at the riddle answers, and having already been denied both the story that would explain the priest's words and any information regarding Pamina's fate, Tamino asks, quietly now, in desperation, "Wann also wird die Decke schwinden?" (When then will the veil be lifted?). In response, the priest sings a somber but clearly structured melody in A minor. It is a striking moment, especially so in a context where we have all but forgotten what real melodies sound like. Also striking is the unison doubling of the voice (only the priest's line has had such an accompaniment, and only once before, when the priest tells Tamino that he shall never find love and virtue as long as death and vengeance are in his heart ["Dich leitet Lieb und Tugend nicht, / Weil Tod und Rache dich entzünden"] at mm. 92–94). The effect is intensified when the cadence in A minor arrives in measure 139, confirming the tonal area of the priest's melody. This is the first clear arrival for seventy measures, and it marks the priest's exit (see example 1.3).

The dialogue ends as it began, with a series of three. The two repetitions of the A-minor melody following the priest's exit, however, set new text and are performed only by the cellos, while offstage voices respond to Tamino's questions. This third threefold repetition also contains two additional instances of repetition of a different kind. The first is a return of material from earlier in the recitative; the two-bar orchestral figure at the priest's exit recalls the moment in the middle of the scene when Tamino turned to go, stressing especially the minor second G-sharp to A (compare the figure marked "x" in example 1.3 with that in example 1.2).[15] The priest's exit is a gesture designed to bring Tamino understanding by leaving him alone, just as detaining him previously was designed to bring him understanding by refusing to let him leave when he was not yet ready to be alone.

Tamino's reaction "O ewige Nacht!" is the second repetition of a different sort. It is, in fact, a reminiscence of something he heard much earlier in the opera. And, as I noted earlier, this phrase is the crux of the entire recognition process. It recalls the Queen's first words to him, in her recitative and aria (No. 4): "O zittre nicht, mein lieber Sohn" (O tremble not, my dear son).[16] (Compare the musical line marked "y" in examples 1.3 and 1.4.) Tamino's exclamation thus involves a recollection from deep within memory. This is precisely what is most characteristic of moments of

---

15. See Wolff, "O ew'ge Nacht!" 244.
16. See Abert, *W. A. Mozart*, 2:656n; and Wolff, "O ew'ge Nacht!" 246.

Example 1.2. *Zauberflöte,* act 1 finale, mm. 100–108.

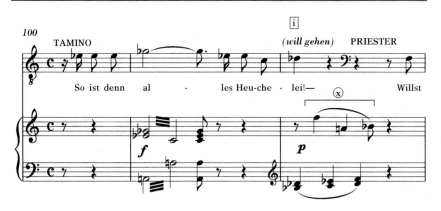

(continued)

Example 1.2. *Continued*

recognition: something already known, the significance of which had never before been apparent, repeats itself and in the process becomes understood. Tamino had thought the Queen to be a force for good, and Sarastro a force for evil. But he now realizes that the reverse is true. Only now does he grasp the significance of what the priest has said, as well as what truly lay behind the Queen's words. In recalling her kindness to him, and the import of her recitative and aria, Tamino remembers, and in remembering now understands for the first time, the truth of what has passed.

The C-major Andante that follows balances the earlier C-major Larghetto entrance of Tamino and the three boys, the two passages serving as a frame for the long accompanied recitative. The irregularity of the recitative section stands in contrast not only to the opera overall but also—and powerfully—to the music immediately preceding and following it. Figure 1.2 offers a graphic representation of this double frame for the recitative. The first frame is marked by tonality, musical style, and the contrast of the surrounding musical context to the recitative, as well as by the parallel of the three boys and the flute as talismans. The recitative is flanked on both sides by C major, by nonrecitative, and by the use of magic—as opposed to reasoning through dialogue.

The second frame is set within the first. The actual dialogue is framed by two of the series of threefold repetitions just described (its midpoint is also marked by a threefold repetition): the three approaches to the gates call the priest forth, and Tamino's questions result in his exit. As we have seen, the third in each series of three brings about an important event: in the first instance the appearance of the priest; in the second, Tamino's decision to remain; and in the last, the newfound knowledge that Pamina is alive. At the priest's exit, however, the layering of repetition, recollection, recognition, and knowledge (the long-sought response that Pamina is alive), and the clear tonal arrival in A minor make this moment especially complex and affecting. The priest's exit does not take place at the third question, but after the first. As figure 1.2 reveals, the threes of the priest's exit (one plus two) mirror the threes of his en-

Example 1.3.   *Zauberflöte*, act 1 finale, mm. 134–53.

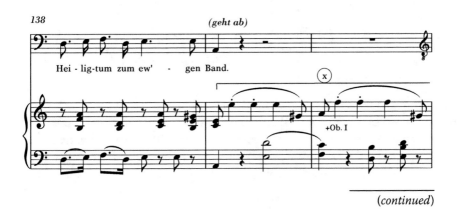

(continued)

Example 1.3. *Continued*

trance (two plus one); the pattern of repetition is not parallel but symmetrical. As I have already suggested, there are dramatic reasons for the priest's leaving Tamino alone to awaken to the truth; nevertheless, the symmetry of the scene is remarkable. Passages of *accompagnato* are not generally thought to possess any particular form, let alone a tightly structured design, yet this recitative exhibits a fluid but balanced

Example 1.3. *Continued*

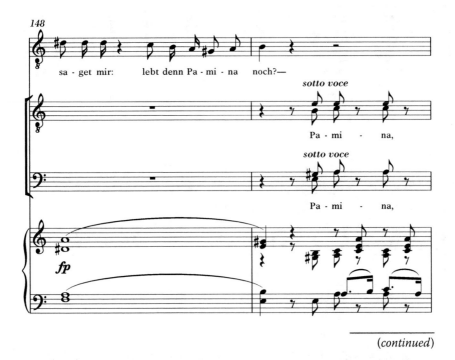

(continued)

internal structure that is supported by its surrounding context (and indeed, as we shall see, by its position in the finale).

Tamino's recognition has come in conjunction with a reversal, and his purpose from this point forward will therefore be different from what it was. It is not an epiphany but rather the first step in a complex process of self-knowledge. The recognition involves repetition at several levels, as I have shown, and also narrative, as critical thinking about recognition predicts. The priest acknowledged the existence of a story that would explain all, but withheld it from Tamino. Tamino has come

Example 1.3.   *Continued*

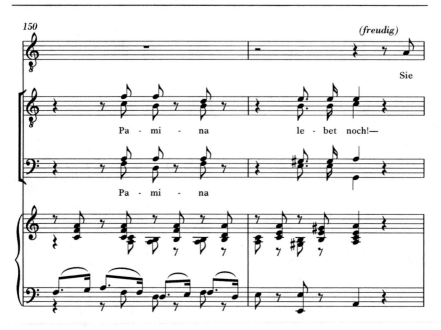

to this stage of knowledge through the operatic events themselves. His two questions at the moment of recognition hold a double implication. The first aspect of recognition, as plot device, is given by "O ewige Nacht! Wann wirst du schwinden?" and the reversal Tamino's realization brings about. The second aspect follows: recognition as a vehicle for themes of knowledge. Tamino's recognition expresses itself as a wish for further enlightenment: "Wann wird das Licht mein Auge finden?" he asks. Although he has attained new awareness, Tamino is still a seeker, now of light and knowledge, and not merely in a personal and limited sense. Confirmation of this perhaps comes when his exit music at the end of the scene recalls his earlier ap-

Example 1.4.   *Zauberflöte*, "O zittre nicht, mein lieber Sohn" (No. 4), mm. 11–12.

KÖNIGIN DER NACHT

O   zitt - re nicht,   mein lie - ber   Sohn,

proach to the gates (compare example 1.5 and "1a" in example 1.1). The question "Wann wird das Licht mein Auge finden?" calls for a second recognition that will be an unfolding and a fulfillment of the first one. The recognition yet to come will be represented in both individual and universal terms, and will be marked by this opera's greatest stage spectacle: the sudden illumination of the stage (one of several special effects for which the Theater auf der Wieden was especially equipped). It will serve as a dramatization for the audience of the whole experience of knowledge, in terms of enlightenment, and will be enacted in the second finale.

Tamino's scene involves the "double character of recognition," in the manner described in the introduction, implying that the act of recognition, as Terence Cave has suggested, mediates the move from issues of form to those of content and back again. Tamino's recognition and the musical events that bring it about cannot be separated from the events of the plot. Confirmed tonality, the repetition of melody (as opposed to motives or gestures), a sustained melodic line in the bass, the promise of a narrative that will reveal all (even though it is withheld), the repetition of a melodic fragment from earlier in the opera that culminates in recognition—all come together powerfully as the events of an operatic plot.

Pamina, Papageno, and the End of the Opera

Recognition in *Zauberflöte* is not only a matter of this single, climactic scene; it is crucial to structure and meaning throughout. Although it would be impractical to draw up an exhaustive list of moments in which recognition is alluded to or enacted on the stage, I do want to emphasize the extent and force of its presence: from the moral lessons Mozart sets in chorale style—when, for example, the three ladies offer the following instruction in the act 1 quintet (No. 5), "Bekämen doch die Lügner alle / Ein solches Schloß vor ihren Mund; / Statt Haß, Verleumdung, schwarzer Galle, / Bestünden Lieb' und Bruderbund" (If all liars had such a lock for their mouths, instead of hatred, slander, black bile, there would be love and brotherhood)—to the structurally important recognition scenes for Tamino, Pamina, and Papageno in the finales. Take, for example, a brief moment of little importance to the action but central to the opera's representation of its high-minded theme: the brief passage in the act 1 finale when Pamina and Papageno, having just charmed Monostatos and his slaves with Papageno's glockenspiel, hear the chorus singing

Figure 1.2.   A double frame for Tamino's dialogue with the priest.

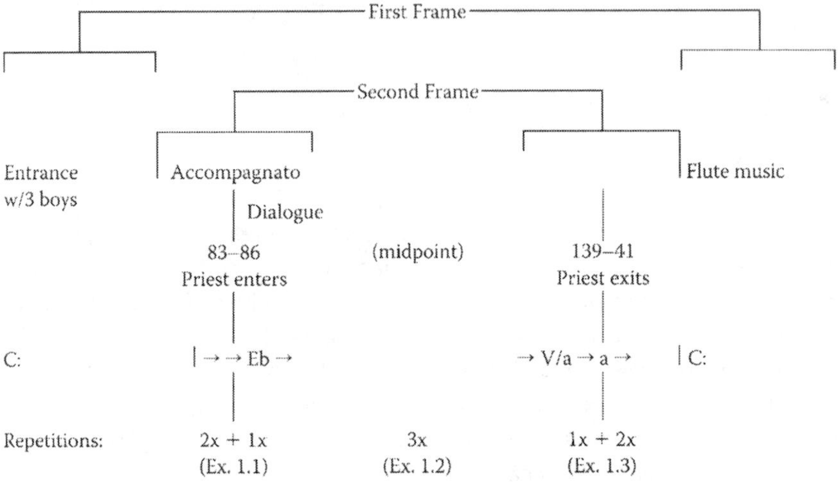

Sarastro's praises in the distance. As the voices grow nearer, Papageno, who is terrified, can think of nothing but his desire to hide:

O wär' ich eine Maus!	If only I were a mouse!
Wie wollt' ich mich verstecken,	I would hide myself,
Wär' ich so klein wie Schnecken,	if only I were as small as a snail,
So kröch' ich in mein Haus.	I would crawl into my house.
Mein Kind, was werden wir nun sprechen?	My child, what shall we say now?

Pamina's response resonates with a significance that reaches beyond the confines of the present stage:

Die Wahrheit! sei sie auch Verbrechen.   The truth! even if it is a crime.

The exchange is dramatized vividly in the music. Papageno moves from G major (the key of the preceding duet section) to C minor, anticipating the worst. But Pamina redirects Papageno's dominant of C minor toward C major on the words "die Wahrheit" (see example 1.6). And it is no accident that her arrival on C major takes place within the context of a finale that both begins and ends in this key. Her "return" to the tonic is both sure-footed and resolute, and thus seems to confirm the import of her words.

The double character of recognition is reflected in many other ways in the opera. Both finales dramatize recognition (though with different emphases), and in this way address themes of knowledge on three levels: first, the individual's pursuit of en-

Example 1.5.   *Zauberflöte*, act 1 finale, mm. 225–27.

lightenment and the happiness it brings; second, the pursuit of happiness without enlightenment; and third, the dramatization of enlightenment as the confrontation of symbolic universals. What is more, as figure 1.3 shows, both finales dramatize knowledge with respect to these three levels in the same order. The act 1 finale falls into three broad sections: first, Tamino's recognition scene; second, Papageno's and Pamina's escape from Monostatos; and third, the entrance of the priests and Sarastro. In the act 2 finale, there are three parallel sections: a recognition scene for Pamina, the scene in which Papageno finds Papagena, and the confrontation of universals in the triumph of light over darkness.

The first sections of both finales are reserved for the most high-minded dramatization of the pursuit of knowledge: Tamino's recognition scene in act 1, and Pamina's triumph over despair and the fire and water trials (which the pair pass together) in act 2. These trials and the completion they represent cannot come until both Tamino and Pamina have declared themselves seekers of enlightenment. The second sections of the finales each focus on the characters belonging to the lower social orders, whose concerns are more earthly. In this part of the act 2 finale, Papageno, who shows little interest in the opportunity he is offered to pursue the elevated enlightenment of Sarastro's order, finds his partner for life. In the equivalent part of the act 1 finale, Pamina, not yet aware of the truth about her own predicament and not yet seeking enlightenment, searches for Tamino in company with Papageno. Her empathy with Papageno—and their mutual desire to find love, something Mozart has already elevated with their duet, "Bei Männern, welche Liebe fühlen" (No. 7)—emphasizes the human bond between the noble and the ordinary, between the enlightened (which she is soon to be) and the unenlightened (which Papageno will choose to remain). In act 2, significantly, Pamina does not appear in the corresponding portion of the finale, where Papageno and Papagena seek a happiness uncomplicated by the higher goals of enlightenment. The third sections of both finales conclude with the representation of universals: Sarastro's first entrance, the meting out of justice to Monostatos, the invitation for Tamino to begin the initiation rites, and eventually the vanquishing of the powers of darkness are all enacted in terms of symbol and ritual.

Example 1.6.   *Zauberflöte,* act 1 finale, mm. 363–74.

Figure 1.3.   Parallel dramatic structures in the *Zauberflöte* finales.

	-1- Pursuit of knowledge		-2- Pursuit of happiness without knowledge	-3- Confrontation of universals: Ignorance vanquished by →	Enlightenment
Finale I:	**Tamino**		**Papageno**	**Sarastro and Priests**	
	3 boys		With Pamina	Join Pamina and Papageno	
	Doubt*		Fear of capture	Tamino enters**	Reconciliation and invitation to trials
	Hope	→ Plays flute	Plays bells	Punishment of Monostatos	Rejoicing
Finale II:	**Pamina** 3 boys	**Trials** Adagio and chorale	**Papageno** Doubt*	**Queen of the Night** Enters with others to surprise Sarastro	Sarastro et al. Sun triumphs over night
	Doubt*	Pamina enters** Flute narrative	3 boys	Plunged into end- less night	Rejoicing
	Hope	Tamino plays flute	Plays bells Papagena and union		

* Narrative is withheld.
** One lover enters to discover the other.

Tamino's recognition scene involves three essential elements that set the pattern for others in which Pamina and Papageno also make discoveries: (1) the presence of the three boys; (2) doubt, overcome by (Socratic) dialogue and culminating in new awareness; and (3) hope, given expression by the playing of the flute (see figure 1.4). Tamino and Pamina, who are destined to be united in marriage, each undergo a moment of great personal struggle. Tamino's despair and new awareness begin the first finale, and Pamina's the second; both involve reasoning through dialogue and withheld narrative. The pattern of action is also the same: the three boys appear; Pamina, in despair, comes to realize through dialogue that Tamino is faithful and resolves to find him; and, as they undergo the trials, the flute is played.[17]

Papageno also has two scenes that follow this pattern, although neither brings him closer to embracing the enlightenment of the order. The first of these makes obvious comic reference to Tamino's scene. In the dialogue before "Ein Mädchen oder Weibchen" (No. 20), Papageno, alone on the stage, despairs and wanders toward a door (the very door through which Tamino has just been led away). As he

17. For an analysis of Pamina's recognition scene, see chapter 2.

Figure 1.4. Recognition scenes for Tamino, Pamina, and Papageno.

Tamino's Despair (finale, act 1)

3 boys	Doubt (→hope)	Plays flute
3 boys give Tamino advice	Tamino tries the gates. "Züruck!"	Thanksgiving
	Dialogue with priest reveals new hope*	Confirmation of what he has learned
(1)	(39)	(160)

Pamina's Despair (finale, act 2)

3 boys	Doubt (→hope)	Trials	Plays flute to pass the trials
3 boys discover Pamina about to commit suicide	Dialogue in which Pamina is given hope and resolves to find Tamino*	Adagio	
		Chorale	
They stop her		Pamina's entrance	
(1)	(94)	(190)	(362 and 378)

Papageno's Despair (before No. 20)

No boys	No doubt (→hope)	Plays bells
Papageno is alone on stage	Told "Züruck!"	Overjoyed by the arrival of some wine
	Dialogue with Speaker	

Papageno's Last Chance (finale, act 2)

Doubt	3 boys (→hope)	Plays bells
Papageno is alone. In despair he plans to hang himself	They appear, stop him, and tell him to play bells*	Hopeful, Papageno plays
		Papagena appears
(413)	(543)	(576)

* Narrative is withheld.

approaches, an offstage voice suddenly calls out "Zurück!" (Back!). The terrified Papageno meets with the same response at another door and, unlike Tamino, abandons hope: "Nun kann ich weder zurück, noch vorwärts!" (Now I can't go back and I can't go on!). The Speaker enters to chastise Papageno, telling him that he will never know the heavenly pleasure of the initiates ("das himmlische Vergnügen der Eingeweihten"). But Papageno feels no remorse; he exclaims, "Je nun, es gibt ja noch mehr Leute meinesgleichen" (Good heavens, there are even more people just like me). Finally, just as Tamino played his flute, Papageno plays his bells, overjo[yed] by the dawning of knowledge or hope, but by the arrival of some wine. Like th[e Ital]ian *buffo*, from whose tradition he is partly derived, Papageno is more focus[ed on] corporeal than cerebral concerns.

In the second finale after the trials, Papageno, in the depths of despair and a[bout] to hang himself because he cannot find Papagena, is given one last chance to c[ome] to awareness, and the three sections of this scene will by now be familiar: the th[ree] boys enter and engage him in dialogue; he is little capable of reason but plays his be[lls]

Figure 1.3. Parallel dramatic structures in the *Zauberflöte* finales.

	-1- Pursuit of knowledge		-2- Pursuit of happiness without knowledge	-3- Confrontation of universals: Ignorance vanquished by →	Enlightenment
Finale I:	**Tamino**		**Papageno**	**Sarastro and Priests**	
	3 boys		With Pamina	Join Pamina and Papageno	
	Doubt*		Fear of capture	Tamino enters**	Reconciliation and invitation to trials
	Hope	→ Plays flute	Plays bells	Punishment of Monostatos	Rejoicing
Finale II:	**Pamina**	**Trials**	**Papageno**	**Queen of the Night**	Sarastro et al.
	3 boys	Adagio and chorale	Doubt*	Enters with others to surprise Sarastro	Sun triumphs over night
	Doubt*	Pamina enters**	3 boys		
		Flute narrative		Plunged into endless night	Rejoicing
	Hope	Tamino plays flute	Plays bells		
			Papagena and union		

* Narrative is withheld.
** One lover enters to discover the other.

Tamino's recognition scene involves three essential elements that set the pattern for others in which Pamina and Papageno also make discoveries: (1) the presence of the three boys; (2) doubt, overcome by (Socratic) dialogue and culminating in new awareness; and (3) hope, given expression by the playing of the flute (see figure 1.4). Tamino and Pamina, who are destined to be united in marriage, each undergo a moment of great personal struggle. Tamino's despair and new awareness begin the first finale, and Pamina's the second; both involve reasoning through dialogue and withheld narrative. The pattern of action is also the same: the three boys appear; Pamina, in despair, comes to realize through dialogue that Tamino is faithful and resolves to find him; and, as they undergo the trials, the flute is played.[17]

Papageno also has two scenes that follow this pattern, although neither brings him closer to embracing the enlightenment of the order. The first of these makes obvious comic reference to Tamino's scene. In the dialogue before "Ein Mädchen oder Weibchen" (No. 20), Papageno, alone on the stage, despairs and wanders toward a door (the very door through which Tamino has just been led away). As he

17. For an analysis of Pamina's recognition scene, see chapter 2.

Figure 1.4. Recognition scenes for Tamino, Pamina, and Papageno.

	Tamino's Despair (finale, act 1)		
3 boys	Doubt (→hope)	Plays flute	
3 boys give Tamino advice	Tamino tries the gates. "Zürück!"	Thanksgiving	
	Dialogue with priest reveals new hope*	Confirmation of what he has learned	
(1)	(39)	(160)	
	Pamina's Despair (finale, act 2)		
3 boys	Doubt (→hope)	Trials	Plays flute
3 boys discover Pamina about to commit suicide	Dialogue in which Pamina is given hope and resolves to find Tamino*	Adagio	to pass the trials
		Chorale	
They stop her		Pamina's entrance	
(1)	(94)	(190)	(362 and 378)
	Papageno's Despair (before No. 20)		
No boys	No doubt (→hope)	Plays bells	
Papageno is alone on stage	Told "Zürück!"	Overjoyed by the arrival of some wine	
	Dialogue with Speaker		
	Papageno's Last Chance (finale, act 2)		
Doubt	3 boys (→hope)	Plays bells	
Papageno is alone. In despair he plans to hang himself	They appear, stop him, and tell him to play bells*	Hopeful, Papageno plays	
		Papagena appears	
(413)	(543)	(576)	

* Narrative is withheld.

approaches, an offstage voice suddenly calls out "Zurück!" (Back!). The terrified Papageno meets with the same response at another door and, unlike Tamino, abandons hope: "Nun kann ich weder zurück, noch vorwärts!" (Now I can't go back and I can't go on!). The Speaker enters to chastise Papageno, telling him that he will never know the heavenly pleasure of the initiates ("das himmlische Vergnügen der Eingeweihten"). But Papageno feels no remorse; he exclaims, "Je nun, es gibt ja noch mehr Leute meinesgleichen" (Good heavens, there are even more people just like me). Finally, just as Tamino played his flute, Papageno plays his bells, overjoyed not by the dawning of knowledge or hope, but by the arrival of some wine. Like the Italian *buffo*, from whose tradition he is partly derived, Papageno is more focused on corporeal than cerebral concerns.

In the second finale after the trials, Papageno, in the depths of despair and about to hang himself because he cannot find Papagena, is given one last chance to come to awareness, and the three sections of this scene will by now be familiar: the three boys enter and engage him in dialogue; he is little capable of reason but plays his bells when told to; and as he plays, Papagena appears. The story of Papageno and Papagena is that of the common folk who find happiness without enlightenment. In Kant's view, all ignorance threatens enlightenment, but in Mozart's fairy-tale world, only a direct attack poses a real threat. The Queen, who is fundamentally opposed to the realm of enlightenment, cannot coexist with it and must be vanquished. Papageno, on the other hand, though unenlightened, might be understood to represent a necessary part of an enlightened universe, the commoner whose lot is improved by the betterment of society as a whole.

The final stage of the representation of knowledge in the opera is the ultimate reversal, the vanquishing of the Queen and her entourage. This is a moment of universal enlightenment, and one of the most remarkable visual spectacles in all opera. As the Queen's C minor is redirected toward E-flat major, the dark stage is suddenly flooded with light. The contrast of styles and of chromatic and diatonic melodic lines, and the turn from minor to major musically represent the metaphoric opposition of dark and light, which is explicitly prescribed in the stage directions: "Sogleich verwandelt sich das ganze Theater in eine Sonne" (All at once, the whole stage is transformed into a sun). The Moor and the Queen exclaim as they descend through a trap door, "Zerschmettert, zernichtet ist unsere Macht, / Wir alle gestürzet in ewige Nacht" (Smashed, destroyed is our power, / We are all plunged into eternal night). Sarastro moralizes, "Die Strahlen der Sonne vertreiben die Nacht, / Zernichten der heuchler erschlichene Macht" (The rays of the sun vanquish the night, / [and] Destroy the ill-gained power of the hypocrites). The ascendance of light is not recognition in terms of the plot. Rather, it is the dramatization of the experience of knowledge for the audience, and the symbolic fulfillment of the enlightenment the opera's recognition scenes have implied. Although Tamino and Pamina achieve enlightenment through the trials by fire and water, they have not been enlightened in our eyes until we see them enter among Sarastro's order, in priestly garb, illuminated by a great sun.

The "Scandal" of Recognition

To return to the subject of the critical literature on *Zauberflöte*, but now from the perspective of recognition as both a crucial dramatic device and a "problem" moment, the fact that Tamino's great recitative scene with the priest has been the source of a well-known critical controversy suddenly takes on a new significance. It has been taken as the key to the story by many—as, in the words of E. M. Batley, "the pivot around which the plot revolves."[18] At the same time, it has also been viewed as the greatest contrivance, the point at which the story and its characters cease to be believable. Brigid Brophy and Eric Werner (and more recent critics as well) follow Dent and Abert in believing that Schikaneder and Mozart changed the original story com-

18. See Webster, "To Understand Verdi and Wagner"; Farnsworth, "Tamino at the Temple's Portals"; and Wolff, "O ew'ge Nacht!"; see also Corse, *Opera and the Uses of Language*, 46–68; Batley, "Textual Unity in *Die Zauberflöte*," 85; and Branscombe, *W. A. Mozart: "Die Zauberflöte*," 205–7.

pletely in midcomposition to avoid replicating a rival production, *Kaspar der Fagotist, oder Die Zauberzither.*[19] According to this theory, which, though based on false premises,[20] has nonetheless been extraordinarily influential, Mozart and Schikaneder originally intended the Queen to be good and Sarastro evil (following the fairy tale from which the story was adapted). However, their change of plan—so the theory goes—necessitated the roles of good and evil to be reversed, creating a break in the plot (at the beginning of the act 1 finale) where their work was interrupted.[21]

How can the same moment be described by so many distinguished commentators as the dramatic crux, and by so many others as the plot's central weakness? One possible answer is that these authors are all responding to the fact of recognition (and its effect on the plot), though they are not seeing the scene as a recognition. What is at issue here is whether plots centered around reversals of this kind can be cohesive. Aristotle, for one, believed that they could be. The contrivance (and reversal) various critics have sensed in *Zauberflöte* is precisely the radical change in understanding inherent in recognition scenes, and, indeed, in fictional plots of any kind. Cave calls this the "scandal" of recognition: recognition is "also a shift *into* the implausible: the secret unfolded lies beyond the realm of the common experience; the truth discovered is 'marvellous' (*thaumaston*, to use Aristotle's term), the truth of fabulous myth or legend."[22] In hindsight, now that Peter Branscombe has shown the "change of plan" theory to have been based on false premises, it appears that the theory was invented—though certainly not self-consciously so—for the purpose of making an excuse for the "implausible" recognition around which Schikaneder and Mozart have fashioned their opera.[23] Tamino's recognition scene is the moment when he first understands his situation. This new understanding naturally reverses his former perceptions of the Queen and of Sarastro (and our perceptions as well), and it alters his quest. The reversal may appear implausible, but this need not be seen as robbing the opera of its dramatic sense or significance, still less as legitimizing the canard that the plot is foolish and unintelligible while the music is intelligible, even unified, and thus able to "redeem" or "transcend" the libretto. Such an artificial division of plot and music is even more implausible than the supposed implausibility it purports to explain.

For all its mysticism, magic talismans, and supernatural happenings, *Zauberflöte,* as we have seen, is really about themes of knowledge. Its primary concern, at multiple levels, is recognition, which represents enlightenment in plot and theme. The opera

---

19. Brophy, *Mozart the Dramatist,* 144–48; Werner, "Leading or Symbolic Formulas in *The Magic Flute,*" 286–93; Dent, *Mozart's Operas,* 218–19; and Abert, *W. A. Mozart,* 2:626–28.

20. See Branscombe, *W. A. Mozart: "Die Zauberflöte,"* 29–34.

21. It should be noted that Schikaneder's and Mozart's indebtedness to the fairy tale "Lulu oder die Zauberflöte" is far more limited than many have supposed. For a discussion of this and other fairy tales in the *Dschinnistan* volumes that influenced the libretto for *Zauberflöte,* see Branscombe, *W. A. Mozart: "Die Zauberflöte,"* 25–27.

22. Cave, *Recognitions,* 1–2.

23. Branscombe, *W. A. Mozart: "Die Zauberflöte,"* 29–34.

is set in a magical world in which enlightenment appears, to borrow Cave's language, both implausible and marvelous. This is the key to the opera. Recognition carries the opera into the implausible; it is the implausible truth that Tamino and Pamina discover that is marvelous, that *is* enlightenment. The opera dramatizes Kant's injunction "Sapere Aude!": to dare to depart from inherited wisdom is to dare to know. If recognition, the marvelous knowledge that comes at the end, is implausible, this only confirms the truth of the enlightenment it brings.

2

❧

Recognition Scenes in Theory and Practice

With its rich overlay of enlightenment metaphor and symbolism, its overt treatment of knowledge as subject—knowledge of a profound, philosophical kind—and its marvelous spectacle at the end, *Die Zauberflöte* might be thought unique in its reliance on recognition in the plot and in its development of recognition as a central theme. Yet all of Mozart's operas dramatize moments of recognition, and in a rich variety of ways. Several of the operas culminate in a moment of climactic recognition, after which things are irrevocably changed; many involve the use of disguise, which must later be discovered; and all involve several scenes in which one or more characters come to some significant realization on stage. What is discovered in each case, of course, is fundamental and particular to each individual artwork. The ideological triumph of Enlightenment principles dramatized in *Zauberflöte* is very different from the exaltation of sentiment found in *La finta giardiniera* or the domestic reconciliation enacted in *Le nozze di Figaro*. What these works have in common, however, is that recognition serves as a key to the drama and brings (or attempts to bring) with it a moral, emotional, philosophical, political, or other form of enlightenment.

The special challenge of approaching recognition in Mozart's operas, as I have already suggested, is to find a way to understand it in terms appropriate to the medium. In the operatic context, in which drama is realized through a combination of text, action, and music (and in which music is generally regarded as *primus inter pares*), recognition, when it comes, is almost always realized in musical terms. As we have seen in the case of Tamino's recognition scene and its implications for *Zauberflöte*, two or more of the following features or circumstances usually figure in the dramatic working out of such moments: (1) moments of recognition are set apart by some musical means; (2) shifts in action are accompanied by shifts of key, texture, melodic line, and overall style and mood;[1] (3) the discovery is accompanied—though

---

1. I have adopted the word "shift" from Else's translation of Aristotle's *Poetics*, where it is used to describe the effects of both peripeteia and recognition: "'Peripety' is a shift of what is being under-

not always immediately—by an explanatory narrative; and (4) most important, perhaps, recognition is brought about or signaled by musical repetition or recollection, just as Tamino remembered and repeated the Queen's melodic phrase.

For example, at the moment in *Don Giovanni* when Donna Anna recognizes Don Giovanni as the man who attacked her in the exchange before her aria "Or sai chi l'onore" (No. 10), there is a shift in texture from *secco* to accompanied recitative at the words, "Don Ottavio, son morta!" Her discovery calls for the narrative of another episode for its explanation, and her account of that fateful night ensues. But sometimes the actual repetition of a certain action or story leads to a new discovery. In *Figaro,* for instance, when the Count interrupts the act 1 trio (No. 7) to tell the little narrative in recitative of how he found Cherubino in Barbarina's room the day before, he reenacts the moment of discovery as he retells the story, lifting the "tablecloth" and once again uncovering Cherubino. With striking visual power in *Zauberflöte,* as we have already seen, Sarastro vanquishes the Queen's darkness, as her tempestuous storm music in C minor (complete with thunder machine) is transformed into the music of Sarastro's stately proclamation in E-flat major. Recognition in opera, as in drama and fiction, often involves the unmasking of a disguise, leading to the revelation, discovery, or recovery of identity. For example, Leporello's disguise is uncovered in the sextet of *Don Giovanni* with a striking change of texture and a deceptive cadence. In the act 4 finale of *Figaro,* the texture, key, and mood change as the Count recognizes the Countess disguised in Susanna's clothing, realizes what he has done, and begs her forgiveness.

In order to explore the complex workings of recognition in Mozart's operas, it is first necessary to focus on critical thinking about the concept in literary genres, and then on the difficult question of its application in the operatic context. Although recognition raises a number of formalist questions that require attention, the workings of recognition scenes cannot be reduced to a formula, nor can the concept of recognition be applied in any mechanical way. My purpose is rather to provide a dramatic and critical context in which to understand these scenes. One way to explore the question of how to apply the critical concept of recognition is to examine the construction of individual recognition scenes to see how they are crucial to the workings of an operatic plot, as I have attempted to do in the case of Tamino's recognition scene in *Zauberflöte* in chapter 1. My aim in this chapter, by contrast, is not so much the illumination or interpretation of any individual work, but rather a consideration of what recognition does, of where it is most and least forcefully dramatized, and why. In chapter 3, I shall turn to the question of how an individual event, such as a recognition scene, functions with respect to the operatic plot as a whole. The larger challenge—to approach recognition in operatic drama more gen-

---

taken to the opposite" (35); and "'recognition' is . . . a shift from ignorance to awareness" (36). "Shift" may be used in the musico-dramatic context with less confusion than Halliwell's word "change" (*Poetics* [11], 43).

erally and involve it in the goals of opera studies—I shall try to address, however briefly, in the afterword.

Recognition in Classical and Contemporary Poetics

As it is used in Aristotle's *Poetics*, the term *anagnôrisis* is primarily concerned with Greek tragedy, though some mention is also made of the genres of comedy and epic. But recognition is integral to more literature and more types of literature than were dreamt of in the *Poetics*, and the term has since been applied to many other genres of diverse literary periods, including Renaissance comedy, Romantic lyric poetry, and the Victorian novel. For these and other reasons, recognition has a long and peculiar history as a literary—and, more particularly, a dramatic—device, and it comes laden with a kind of critical baggage that is not easily unpacked. In his *Recognitions: A Study in Poetics*, Terence Cave devotes over two hundred pages to what he calls "initial exercises," in which he offers a magisterial treatment of the origin, history, translation, and usage of the term, with extensive consideration of its reception, interpretation, and rehabilitation in commentaries ranging from the literature of antiquity to present-day poststructuralism.[2] For the present study, although the initial exercises need not be as strenuous, it does seem important to consider the nature of recognition both as a plot device and as a subject for poetics.

Although the subject of recognition has in the course of its curious history engendered interpretation and discussion of various kinds, there is no overarching—let alone consistent—theory of it, even in Aristotle. The disagreement that has pervaded the literature may be traced in large measure back to the ellipses and ambiguities of the original text as we have inherited it. Philosophers, playwrights, poets, historians, and literary critics of many different periods have produced so many conflicting translations, editions, and interpretations that it is almost impossible to conceive of the text we call the *Poetics* as a single text. The resulting texts have become part of the dialogue, spawning other translations, readings, and misreadings, even to the point at which ideas that all but contradict the letter of the original document have come to be regarded as central tenets of Aristotle's argument. (One of the most influential of these misreadings, for example, is the shift of attention that began with Gotthold Lessing in the eighteenth century, from recognition and peripeteia to pathos, which came to be regarded as the hallmark of good drama. In fact, however, pathos—the third of the three constituent parts of the plot—is the one about which Aristotle says the least.) Were it not for this complicated reception history, however, the text we call the *Poetics* might well hold considerably less influence. In the context of literary theory, recognition has thus been defined and understood in different ways at different times. Similarly, it has repeatedly been redefined (and even recreated) to apply

---

2. Cave, *Recognitions*, 4.

lent."[14] Like the recognition of the first type, this type is weak in Aristotle's view because it is brought about by the poet. In neither the first nor the second type is recognition brought about by the events themselves.

The third type is the recognition of memory and "may depend on the sight of something," or on hearing something.[15] This is perhaps the most common type of recognition in poetry, fiction, and drama, and is also important to theories that make use of the idea of recognition—psychoanalysis, for example. The crucial element here is repetition (as we saw in the introduction), which recalls some former event that is reenacted as it is repeated and is now understood with new awareness.

The fourth type, reason, implies the protagonist's use of deductive reasoning in a way implied by or natural to the plot. Aristotle's example comes from the *Libation-Bearers:* "someone like Electra has come, and there is no one like her other than Orestes, so it is he who has come."[16] Here the protagonist comes to awareness through the piecing together of information he has gained in the course of the action. This example and others of its type emphasize the real difficulty one encounters in attempting to establish such categories since all recognitions make use of reasoning. This category seems to require that recognition is triggered primarily by reasoning, but one cannot overlook the presence of deductive reasoning when the nurse identifies her master by means of his scar, or Oedipus recognizes himself in the messenger's report. Indeed, reasoning might be thought to be a vital component of all recognition scenes, particularly those involving the discovery or recovery of knowledge, as, for example, in *Zauberflöte.* The importance of this second-best type, recognition through reasoning (*sullogismos*), was especially prized by the Renaissance Aristotelians.[17]

Fifth and finest is the type of recognition represented by *Oedipus,* which I discussed briefly in the introduction: "The best of all recognitions is the type which arises from the events themselves, where the emotional impact comes about through a probable sequence of action. There are examples in Sophocles' *Oedipus,* and in *Iphigenia.* . . . Such instances alone avoid contrived tokens."[18] As we have already seen, there are two criteria for this type of recognition: that it, in Aristotle's words, "arises from the events themselves," and that it be accompanied by a peripeteia, as explained in chapter 11 of the *Poetics.*

But how does Aristotle's use of the recognition in *Oedipus* as paradigmatic compare to a recognition that could never have been imagined at the time of the *Poetics*—for example, Tamino's recognition scene in *Zauberflöte?* There can be no doubt that Aristotle prepares the way for a consideration of recognition scenes of all kinds,

14. *Poetics* (16), 49.
15. *Poetics* (16), 49.
16. *Poetics* (16), 49.
17. Cave, *Recognitions,* 72–78.
18. *Poetics* (16), 49–50.

even though his thinking clearly favors the recognition of persons and particularly the discovery of blood ties, which of course Tamino's recognition is not. Furthermore, his division of recognition scenes into types provides a means of identifying and evaluating individual scenes and, by extension, whole artworks. Yet his typology and categorization cannot be strictly maintained. A recognition by token will necessarily involve some deductive reasoning; a recognition brought about by the events of the plot will often involve either recollection or reasoning; and more generally, a recognition of any kind—no matter how contrived it may seem—might be thought to be brought about by the events of the plot, as it is more generally conceived, simply because it takes place in the course of the action. For these and other reasons, it would be pointless to try to base an understanding of recognition scenes in opera on Aristotle's categories.

His five types do, however, have direct bearing on the literature from which he draws his examples, and which his theory attempts to explicate and evaluate. Aristotle's typology seems precisely designed to fit the practice he knew. In this way he provides a model for any attempt to apply the ideas of the *Poetics* to opera: a consideration of recognition scenes must be based on the practice found in the body of works being considered. Tamino's recognition scene therefore should be related in some ways to other recognition scenes in Mozart, not just to those central to Aristotle's (or any other) typology. In other words, there must be a clear and demonstrable compatibility between theory and practice. There is no question that Aristotle's *Poetics* is oriented toward tragedy, although he extends his concepts to comedy and epic.[19] In a broader context in which neither tragedy nor the discovery of family ties is the norm, however, the idea of recognition has developed differently, such that it is the spirit rather than the letter of his treatise that applies. Tamino's recognition is comparable to Aristotle's finest type because it is brought about by the events themselves and involves peripeteia, as Aristotle requires of good drama. At the same time, however, Tamino's recognition is very different in kind from the discovery of family ties that Aristotle favors (more on this below). Aristotle, therefore, is essential for considering recognitions, but the theory in the *Poetics* cannot be regarded as restrictive.

Two further aspects of the *Poetics* have direct bearing on the project at hand. The first of these has to do with the shift of fortune brought about by recognition and peripeteia. This shift moves in one of two directions: from good fortune to bad, as in the case of the *Oedipus* story, or from bad to good, as in the case of *Zauberflöte* and almost all eighteenth-century opera. Much of the argument in the *Poetics* supports the move from good to ill fortune. But later in the *Poetics* Aristotle speaks in favor of plots that mark the opposite shift. And here a question arises that has long been the subject of scholarly debate and will likely never admit of solution. How can the finest plots move in the direction of good fortune when the finest recognitions

---

19. See *Poetics* (3, 5, and 22–26), 33, 36, and 56–65, respectively.

move in the direction of bad fortune?[20] In chapter 14 Aristotle suggests a second ty-pology for evaluating drama, namely, his "modes" of action. Here he again offers a ranked categorization of types of acts, asserting that the finest type of action in tragedy is that in which recognition *prevents* the tragic deed and thus marks a shift from ill to good fortune.[21] This is of course a shift in the opposite direction from that of the paradigmatic *Oedipus* story. Thus there is a discrepancy between the finest type of recognition (to act in ignorance and recognize it later in conjunction with a peripeteia) and the finest mode of acting (to be *about* to act in ignorance and to rec-ognize it in time not to act). There is a similar discrepancy between the finest mode of acting, which brings about a shift of fortune from bad to good, and Aristotle's bias in favor of plots that dramatize the shift from good to bad fortune.[22] To escape ig-norance in time not to perform the deed will necessarily bring about the opposite of the more desirable shift—precisely the move from bad to good fortune.

It is obvious that this system is complex—to the point of contradiction—even with respect to the literature it was designed to comment upon. Aristotle's methods of evaluating both recognition and the modes of action possible within plots are more valuable as ways of making observations about dramatic action than as a means of evaluating whole works. If taken as a set of useful observations rather than as a set of laws, his system may be drawn upon and applied in a flexible way. The questions he raises do not circumscribe and define the recognition scenes one finds in later lit-eratures, but they do offer a way to begin considering recognition scenes of all kinds, and they emphasize the ways in which recognition scenes are centered on the loss and recovery of knowledge. These recognitions, like the ones of family identity that Aristotle favored, lie at the very heart of the works in which they play a part.

The second point, which also involves a contradiction, is central to the way in which recognition narratives work and fundamental to critical thinking about recog-nition in any context. It concerns the development of epic, which, Aristotle says, though it differs in length, meter, and narrative mode, is otherwise similar to tragedy. Thus in chapter 24, he asserts that the epic plot, like the tragic one, may be either simple or complex and involves the same elements of plot: "For epic has equal need of reversals, recognitions and scenes of suffering."[23] Aristotle's examples are Homer's two epic poems: "the *Iliad* in the categories of the 'simple' and the poem of suffering, the *Odyssey* in those of the complex (using recognition throughout) and the poem of character."[24] The epic form, "on account of its use of narrative, can include many simultaneous parts," and a "variety of episodes."[25] It thus possesses the ability to rep-

---

20. See Cave, *Recognitions*, 36.

21. See *Poetics* (14), 45–47; see also the commentaries by Halliwell (131–39) and Else (40–42 and note 99).

22. *Poetics* (13), 45.

23. *Poetics* (24), 59.

24. *Poetics* (24), 59.

25. *Poetics* (24), 59. The operatic equivalent is the musical drama based on a multiple plot, a dis-cussion of which follows in chapter 3 of this volume.

resent more parts of the action than the ideal "unitary," or unified, drama.[26] The development of this variety of episodes and the extension of the story well beyond the confines of the dramatic structure necessarily require the poet to spin out his narrative in a way very different from that common to tragedy and comedy. (This is, of course, precisely the problem Wagner ran into in writing his *Ring* cycle, which attempts by means of the *leitmotiv* to solve the dramatic problem of combining the epic and the dramatic.)

In a narrative as long as the *Odyssey* (or *David Copperfield* or *Moby Dick*), recognition cannot have the same status in the early episodes as it will in later ones, for if it did the truth revealed by recognition in the early episodes would end the story. The consequence is that recognition scenes in epics are often false or partial ones, in which the knowledge gained is untrue, or at least misleading. Aristotle explains the technique with a bow to the great epic poet of his time: "It is above all Homer who has taught other epic poets the right way to purvey falsehoods. What is involved here is a kind of fallacy."[27] These false recognitions are a necessity of the long narrative forms, for they are the chief means by which an author may extend the story over many diverse episodes and postpone the crucial, or climactic, recognition. This is as true for epics as for narrative poems, novels, and even multiplot dramas. Cave offers a summary better adapted to modern literature: "Paralogism [false reasoning], then, is the supreme confidence trick. It allows the charade of 'consequential action,' of narrative motivation, to culminate in an astonishing reversal which the audience accepts as logical although it is based on a fallacy."[28] Herein lies another contradiction: epic recognition sanctions false reasoning. The conclusion is as inevitable as it is vital to the study of recognition: "The problem is one created by the confrontation of philosophical argument with improbable fictions. Anagnorisis cannot be fully assimilated to logic: the attempt to tame it produces warps and lapses, paradoxes and paralogisms."[29] We have returned, albeit by a circuitous route, to the conclusion of chapter 1—namely, that recognition marks the shift into the implausible. Recognition will not be governed by the logic of the plot, but rather will strike out, overcoming the restrictions of structure and plausibility to realize the implausible or marvelous—to become fiction.

When Byron comments on Aristotle's rules in his irreverent *Don Juan,* he anticipates a new poetics of his own devising, which he proposes to call "Longinus o'er a Bottle, / Or, Every Poet his *own* Aristotle."[30] But there is much truth in Byron's jest. To a great extent, Mozart and his librettists may be understood to constitute their

---

26. "Unity," or the notion of a "unitary and complete action," is a central tenet of Aristotle's thinking (*Poetics* [8], 40).

27. *Poetics* (24), 60. Else translates this "fallacy" as "false inference" (65).

28. Cave, *Recognitions*, 43.

29. Cave, *Recognitions*, 43.

30. Byron, *Don Juan*, I.cciv.

own Aristotle. At the same time, although Aristotle's orientation toward blood ties and the specifics of his five types are not directly applicable in this different context, the general tenor of his argument holds. Recognition scenes and the reversals they usually entail are fundamental to stories of every kind. Studying how these scenes function is the key to understanding the larger works as coherent wholes. Recognition is not merely brought about by the events of the plot; rather, it is the culmination of a process that is both product and producer of change. After the detailed exploration of examples to follow in the remainder of this chapter and later chapters, we may perhaps begin to decide with what degree of success Mozart became his own Aristotle.

Recognitions of Identity in Mozart

Bearing in mind what we have learned about recognition—that it often marks not only a shift in dramatic action but a narrative problem in stories, that false or partial recognitions are a necessary component of stories that do not observe the "unity of action" of the Greek tragedies, and that recognition was first defined by Aristotle in his *Poetics* for application to a specific set of literatures—let us return to its application to Mozart and late eighteenth-century opera. Authors in this period were well aware of the function and history of recognition scenes in dramatic plots, as we saw in the introduction. Mozart and Da Ponte, in adapting the extraordinary recognition scene in *Figaro*, seized on and emphasized the suspicion of recognition Beaumarchais had constructed in his play. Suspicion of recognition as a device was characteristic of French writers of the Neoclassical period who struggled to reconcile its "marvelous" effects with the difficulties it necessarily imposed. Some authors suggest, as André Dacier does, for example, in his *La Poetique d'Aristotle*, that playwrights of his day "have rarely used recognition as a means of denouement."[31] As Cave has shown, however, the "decline of recognition" in this period is found more in critical theory than in practice. Metastasio inveighs against the "systems" of Aristotle's *Poetics* but does not refrain from centering his libretti on recognition scenes.[32] Recognition remains essential to plots in the eighteenth century but is adapted to new philosophical and literary ideals. Diderot, for instance, advises against the use of suspense: "Let all the characters be ignorant of one another's identity, if you wish; but let the spectator know them all."[33] In Mozart's operas (and in the operas of his contemporaries), recognition is adapted in a number of ways that reflect the ideals and concerns of their age.

I shall turn first to the sort of recognition Aristotle favored, the recognition of persons, which serves to reveal hidden or unknown identity. In this way, it will be-

---

31. Cited in Cave, *Recognitions*, 120. For a discussion of recognition in the critical thought of this period, see 84–143.
32. Cited in Cave, *Recognitions*, 125.
33. Cited in Cave, *Recognitions*, 128.

come immediately apparent how very different the plots of Mozart's operas are from those Aristotle considers, and, in consequence, which aspects of the *Poetics* are the most illuminating and which the most problematic in this sphere. Of special interest to Aristotle are those scenes in which family ties are revealed, as in the paradigmatic stories of Odysseus and Oedipus. But in Mozart's operas, we may observe, as Cave has in the realm of literature, "the fading of the classic set of family recognitions (recognition of persons, as in *Oedipus* and the *Odyssey*) into a wider set of plots structured explicitly in terms of the loss and recovery of knowledge."[34] The tendency to celebrate individual discoveries of feeling (especially love), to favor striving for knowledge over inherited wisdom, and to center plots on themes of enlightened governance in both the political and the domestic spheres in Mozart's operas foregrounds recognition in a new way.

Family recognitions do occur in Mozart's operas, as when Marcellina and Bartolo recognize Figaro as their long-lost illegitimate son, or when Idomeneo and Idamante recognize each other on the rocky shore of Crete. But more prevalent are recognitions of identity that do not turn on the discovery of family ties—for example, when Sandrina in *Giardiniera* is recognized by her former lover to be the Marchesa Violente, whom he thought dead, or when Donna Anna recognizes Don Giovanni as the man who attacked her, or when Tamino and Pamina first meet and recognize in each other the partner of a future (and a better) life with the words "Er ist's! / Sie ist's!" (It's he! / It's she!). It is striking, however, that of the five scenes just mentioned, none may be regarded as the central climax of its surrounding drama. Anna's recognition of Don Giovanni and Tamino's and Pamina's mutual recognition are important moments in the development of their respective plots, but neither serves as the greatest point of dramatic conclusion or reversal. Similarly, those in *Giardiniera* and *Idomeneo* serve primarily as essential catalysts to later action, and the recognition of Figaro by a spatula-shaped birthmark on his arm, though it unquestionably serves a necessary plot function, seems to have been included at least in part as a clever play on the conventions of recognition.

Thus the recognition of persons, even when it participates in the central climax (as it does in the finales of *Figaro* and *Così fan tutte*), and whether it is a recognition of family ties or not, is de-emphasized in favor of recognitions of other kinds—recognitions of principles, feelings, social and human verities, and so on. Take, for example, the scene in *Idomeneo* in which father and son discover each other's identity. To the extent that it represents a recognition of identity that reveals close family ties, it is similar in some respects to examples cited in the *Poetics*. (This is hardly surprising, of course, since the opera and the plays upon which the libretto was based are all derived from the Greek legend of Idomeneus.)[35] At the same time, the way in which it functions in the drama overall does not finally conform to what Aristotle says about

34. Cave, *Recognitions*, 8–9.
35. See Heartz, *Mozart's Operas*, 1–13.

the significance of family ties. For these reasons, this scene makes a particularly good starting point for a consideration of how and why recognition is conceived differently in Mozart's late eighteenth-century poetics.

In the course of a sudden and violent tempest in which Idomeneo, his ship, and his men are almost lost, Idomeneo makes a vow to Neptune that he will sacrifice the first man he meets on the shore if Neptune will save him and his entourage. Neptune does what is asked of him, but no sooner has Idomeneo set foot on the shore than he begins to reflect on the peculiar nature of his vow: the cost of his rescue will be an innocent life. In fact, it is his own son, Idamante, who now appears on the shore searching for news of his father, whom he knew to be on this ship. At first, father and son do not recognize each other, for it has been many years since Idomeneo's departure, but midway through their recitative Idamante identifies himself as the son of Idomeneo. The event is akin to Aristotle's second poorest type of recognition, for Idamante simply blurts out his identity. Still, it is a necessary plot spring. Were the first man Idomeneo encountered not his own son, he might never come to hate the vow he made and to rethink the precepts by which he rules.[36]

Recognition here is almost exactly as Aristotle describes: "a change from ignorance to knowledge, bringing the characters into either a close bond, or enmity, with one another, and concerning matters which bear on their prosperity or affliction."[37] At the instant Idamante exclaims that Idomeneo is his father, the orchestra comes in all at once with a vigorous Presto on D major (see example 2.1). Julian Rushton and Daniel Heartz have both drawn attention to this moment, and the problematic implications of this recognition scene as a dramatic event become apparent when one considers how strikingly different their views of it are. Here is Rushton:

> Idamante enters . . . and approaches the stranger on the shore to offer comfort and seek news. Recognition is almost unbearably slow, the dialogue punctured by asides. It emerges that the boy has lost his father. The older man sighs; Idamante asks if he knew Idomeneo. The king does not identify himself but seeks a reason for the boy's interest. As Idamante says "He is my father" the orchestra initiates a violent Presto.[38]

Contrary to Rushton's suggestion that "recognition is almost unbearably slow," Heartz recreates the moment in his prose as anything but slow. He takes D as the "keynote" in *Idomeneo* and argues that this moment is vital to the opera's structure and meaning:

> There is often a special drama inherent in the returns to the keynote. Mozart saves it for crucial moments such as the Recognition Scene, Act 1 scene 10. When Idamantes finally, after a long dialogue of questions on both sides,

36. See Till, *Mozart and the Enlightenment*, 67.
37. *Poetics* (11), 43.
38. Rushton, *W. A. Mozart: "Idomeneo,"* 12.

Example 2.1. *Idomeneo,* recitative, "Spiagge romite" (I, x), mm. 1–4.

says of Idomeneus "E il padre mio!", D major arrives with an orchestral tutti, *presto e forte* (NMA, p. 109). The string arpeggios rocketing up to high D are the same as in the overture (pp. 6–7). The similarity of the sonority, if not the pitch, ought to tell every last listener that this is, ye Gods! the keynote ("Spietatissimi Dei!", responds Idomeneus just after the D major arpeggio).[39]

Heartz's reading of the moment is persuasive, and he goes on to connect the keynote to several prominent moments in the opera, including Idomeneo's act 2 aria "Fuor del mar ho un mar in seno" (No. 12), as well as his recitative confession during the storm, "Eccoti in me, barbaro nume!"

Yet, in spite of the forcefulness of the orchestra and the striking interjection of the keynote, one feels that Rushton's reading is also in some sense right. Although this recognition is without doubt important to the drama of *Idomeneo* yet to unfold and exhibits musical connections to earlier and later moments, in its placement and

---

39. Heartz, "Tonality and Motif in *Idomeneo,*" 384.

working out, this moment is in certain respects underplayed, which is precisely what Rushton's reaction reflects. Recognition scenes, particularly the ones that uncover family ties in Aristotle's *Poetics*, usually come as the culmination of a complex plot, bringing about the climax of the drama and a release of dramatic tension. Idomeneo's and Idamante's recognition scene is not of this kind. Indeed, the opera is hardly begun; this moment is the very springboard for which the plot has been waiting. The full significance of this discovery is understood at this point by neither father nor son. (And one cannot help but observe here how different this moment is from the recognition in *Oedipus*, when, after the herdsman has revealed that the child he had saved many years before had been given to him by Jocasta, Oedipus comes to understand who he is and all he has done.) Contrary to Aristotle's preference, this scene is not brought about by the events themselves; it is rather a part of a larger recognition process that culminates in later scenes, including Idomeneo's crisis and confession in the storm and the final *deus ex machina* in which love and virtue triumph.

Thus while Heartz rightly shows the importance of this early recognition scene to the opera as a whole, Rushton correctly suggests that this recognition does not result in the climax one often expects from recognition scenes. It is the forerunner of discoveries yet to come. In studying this moment of familial recognition, we discover how very different are Mozart's recognitions of family identity from Aristotle's. In *Oedipus*, the moment at which filial identity is revealed is the dramatic and moral climax. Birthright, it might be argued, is *the* key to the Oedipus story. In *Idomeneo*, however, the scene that reveals son to father only begins to point to the emotional and moral content of the work. The more significant recognition—the nature of Idomeneo's terrible mistake—has yet to unfold. And herein lies the interest of this scene in the present context, for, perhaps more than any other in Mozart's oeuvre, it demonstrates the shift that Cave speaks of from recognitions of family identity to ones that emphasize the loss and recovery of knowledge. Here then is confirmation (if confirmation is needed) that while Aristotle's general concept of recognition can be usefully applied to Mozart, it is the spirit rather than the letter of his observations that proves most illuminating. What is more, as we have already seen in the case of Tamino's climactic recognition in the act 1 finale of *Zauberflöte*, a recognition scene need not be of the type Aristotle prized to produce the effect within the drama that he valued most highly.

For comparison, let us now turn to a moment in which the recognition of persons reveals something other than family ties. Since its larger recognition drama is already familiar from chapter 1, I have chosen an example from *Zauberflöte:* the moment at which, although they have never met before, Tamino and Pamina instinctively recognize each other in the act 1 finale. By this time their mutual affection is all but assured, for Tamino has already fallen in love with Pamina's portrait (the subject of "Dies Bildnis ist bezaubernd schön" [No. 3]), and Pamina with Papageno's description of the noble prince who has come to rescue her. In this way, the first encounter of these would-be lovers is prepared as a recognition scene. The feelings of love they earlier imagined become manifest at this moment, near the end of act 1, in which they now know each other immediately. As Monostatos enters with Tamino, Pamina exclaims, "Er ist's!" (It's he!). Tamino responds by repeating her exact thought—and music—a fourth below, "Sie ist's!" (It's she!), and they continue exchanging both musical figures and text until their imitation melds into homorhythm and finally they embrace (see example 2.2).

The words here are important; the verb "sein" itself is the mark of recognition, the key to identity. Pamina does not exclaim, as she might have, "At last, I see him!" or more simply, "Tamino!" but recognizes her prince with the thought, "It *is* he." Their next lines are also paired and rhymed: "Ich glaub' es kaum!" (I can scarcely believe it!) and "Es ist kein Traum!" (It is not a dream!). They continue as if of one mind—

PAMINA
Es schling' mein Arm sich um ihn her,   I will wrap my arms around him,
Und wenn es auch mein Ende wär'.   even if it means my death.

TAMINO
Es schling' mein Arm sich um sie her,   I will wrap my arms around her
Und wenn es auch mein Ende wär'.   even if it means my death.

—until, on the last line, they sing the same text to the same melody. The recognition here is realized in text, action, and music. Though brief, it is a remarkably vivid moment, for the music suggests that these two individuals who have never met know each other as well as each knows herself or himself.

At the parallel moment in the act 2 finale, Pamina enters to discover Tamino and the two armed men. This moment, too, is a recognition in miniature, a reunion that seems to reflect and grow out of the earlier encounter. Once again in F major one lover enters to discover the other, and both express their joy with shared text and music. While in the parallel place in act 1 each lover recognizes and identifies the other with the words "It's he/she," this second moment unfolds that earlier one to reveal the confirmation of their affection and its attendant sense of belonging: "Tamino mein! O welch ein Glück!" (My Tamino! O what good fortune!), to which Tamino responds, taking her words and music, "Pamina mein! O welch ein Glück!"[40] The musical setting recalls the earlier exchange, though in a different meter; compare, for example, Pamina's "Ich glaub' es kaum" and Tamino's "Es ist kein Traum" with their settings of "O welch ein Glück!" (see examples 2.2 and 2.3). This moment in the act 2 finale serves as both the fulfillment of the promise of the first recognition and a prediction of a deeper knowledge yet to come—when Tamino and Pamina will come to know each other as man and wife. The elective affinity here is complemented

40. See Webster, "Cone's 'Personae' and the Analysis of Opera"; and Bauman, "At the North Gate," especially 278–86.

Example 2.2. *Zauberflöte,* act 1 finale, mm. 445–61.

(continued)

Example 2.2.   *Continued*

Example 2.3.   *Zauberflöte*, act 2 finale, mm. 277–85.

later in the same finale by the one between Papageno and Papagena: Mozart and Schikaneder convey both the surprise and significance of recognition by having each lover struggle to utter the other's name, "Pa-Pa-Pa-Pa-Pa-Papagena"/"Pa-Pa-Pa-Pa-Pa-Pa-Papageno."

Although recognition serves the common goal of revealing identity in each case, these scenes from *Idomeneo* and *Zauberflöte* could hardly be more dissimilar. It is not merely that the nature of the identity discovered is different (kinship in one case, love in the other), but that identity functions within the two plots with different emphases and in different ways. In the opera seria, father and son do not at first recognize each other, and even after they do they remain unable to communicate with or understand one another (not only for the remainder of the scene, but for most of the opera). What recognition reveals here is birthright and its legacy; its significance derives from a familial and political context. What is more, the recognition of blood relation, which might seem to be a recognition of the highest order, is, in fact, only preparatory to the real drama of *Idomeneo*, which turns on the discoveries Idomeneo makes later about the kind of ruler he would like to be. In *Zauberflöte*, by contrast, Tamino and Pamina, though they have never met and are not related, recognize each other instantly and immediately appear to be one in mind and heart. They discover who they are not in familial but in social and psychological terms, and the emphasis is on who they are to become. The key to understanding therefore lies not in birthright or social identity, but in the acquisition of philosophical and sentimental knowledge. Pamina, we learn from Sarastro at the beginning of act 2, is destined for Tamino, and their union is as important to the future of the temple and the precepts for which it stands as Tamino's trials of initiation. Thus the trials and the philosophical knowledge they represent are inextricably tied to the more fundamental human experience the lovers' union implies. It is only after passing the trials of fire and water that Tamino and Pamina, secure in their newly gained knowledge, are free to become man and wife and to rule jointly in the enlightened temple.

Like *Zauberflöte*, Mozart's first German opera for Vienna de-emphasizes the recognition of persons in favor of that of enlightened principles. In order to do this, Stephanie and Mozart deliberately removed a crucial recognition of family ties from Christoph Friedrich Bretzner and Johann André's *Belmont und Constanze* of 1780 upon which they based their own libretto.[41] As a result, they altered the climax and dénouement of the story in a profound and striking way. Near the end of *Die Entführung aus dem Serail*, Belmonte and Pedrillo are thwarted in their attempt to rescue Constanze and Blonde; the Pasha arrives to discover their plot to escape. When Belmonte gives the name of his family and offers to pay any ransom that might be desired for his and Constanze's freedom, the Pasha learns that Belmonte is none other than the son of the commandant of Oran, who years earlier had robbed him of his own beloved, his honor, and his wealth. The Pasha realizes his good fortune; he holds in his hands the fate of his most hated enemy's son. And his first inclination is to have his revenge: "Wie er mit mir verfahren ist, will ich mit dir verfahren" (As he dealt with me, so shall I deal with you).

The Pasha finally chooses enlightened benevolence over impassioned revenge, however. He returns in the last scene to free his prisoners, despite Belmonte's statement that retribution in kind would be warranted: "Kühle deine Rache an mir, tilge das Unrecht, so mein Vater dir angetan;—ich erwarte alles, und tadle dich nicht" (Take your revenge on me; correct this wrong, which my father did to you. I am prepared for everything and cannot criticize you). But revenge is neither a theme of this opera nor a goal of its plot. In explaining his decision, the Pasha provides the enlightened moral of the opera:

Ich habe deinen Vater viel zu sehr verabscheut, als daß ich je in seine Fußstapfen treten könnte. Nimm deine Freiheit, nimm Konstanzen, segle in dein Vaterland, sage deinem Vater, daß du in meiner Gewalt warst, daß ich dich freigelassen, um ihm sagen zu können, es wäre ein weit größer Vergnügen, eine erlittene Ungerechtigkeit durch Wohltaten zu vergelten, als Laster mit Lastern [zu] tilgen.

41. See Bauman, *W. A. Mozart: "Die Entführung aus dem Serail,"* 6–11, 32–35, and 36–61.

I hold your father in far too much contempt ever to follow in his footsteps. Take your freedom, take Constanze, sail back to your fatherland, and tell your father that you were in my power and that I set you free so that you could tell him that it is a greater pleasure to reward a suffered injustice with good deeds than to repay vice with vice.

Although the earlier recognition disclosed the identity of Belmonte, this final scene is the more important recognition moment. In it the Pasha delivers his speech of enlightened clemency. Most striking here is the fact that the Pasha decides in favor of forgiveness and leniency in spite of his captive's identity, not because of it. As it did in *Idomeneo,* the recognition of persons takes a place of secondary importance to the discovery of the Enlightenment tenets and principles that support the opera's main action and theme.

The full extent to which Stephanie and Mozart de-emphasize recognitions of identity in their opera becomes apparent only when one compares their libretto to Bretzner's *Belmont und Constanze.* At the end of this earlier version, Belmont is revealed to be the Pasha's long-lost son (who had been left at a monastery when he was only four years old). The Pasha's forgiveness is therefore motivated entirely by the discovery of blood relation. He spares not his enemy's but his *own* son. The enlightened benevolence that defines Stephanie's and Mozart's opera is not at issue at all. This substitution in *Entführung* of enlightened goodwill for familial feeling was judged by at least one contemporary critic to be even more contrived and unlikely than the recognition of kinship. Johann Friedrich Schink, who reviewed the premiere of *Entführung,* found the Pasha's forgiveness of his enemy's son to be a much nobler conclusion than the recognition in Bretzner's version, but "incomparably more unnatural." Schink goes on to attribute the change in the story to fashion: "In general these endless acts of magnanimity are a wretched thing, and in fashion on scarcely a single stage any more save the one here. And one can almost be sure that such a work containing handsome feats of magnanimity, generosity, recognition, and forgiveness will make a great splash, even if these things are brought about in the most unnatural way."[42]

While Schink regrets the change of plot, regarding the opera's climactic recognition scene as a problem, we might be inclined to judge it less harshly. The two versions of the story center on different improbabilities. Bretzner's recognition provides the Pasha with a motive for forgiveness and brings about a shift from bad to good fortune. The recovery of a long-lost son easily explains the action, but the improbability strains belief. Stephanie's recognition, by contrast, provides the Pasha with a further motive for revenge. In this context, the Pasha's morally enlightened decision represents a reversal that, though it too strains belief, dramatizes the ideal of forgiveness, as well as the shift from bad to good fortune, in a much more compelling

---

42. Cited in Bauman, *W. A. Mozart, "Die Entführung aus dem Serail,"* 34.

manner. These two endings represent very different ways of employing recognition and illuminate the shift from the recognition of persons to the discovery of knowledge that I mentioned earlier. The ending of *Belmont und Constanze* is a tried and true dénouement: what had appeared to be the inevitable conclusion toward which the events were pointing is averted at the last moment by the revelation of hidden identity. The ending of *Entführung* reconfigures recognition to dramatize the efficacy of the opera's theme of enlightened benevolence, and might be thought in this way to anticipate the powerful final scenes of *Zauberflöte* and *La clemenza di Tito*.

What does this brief consideration of recognitions of identity in *Idomeneo, Zauberflöte,* and *Entführung* reveal about the relevance of Aristotle's poetics to Mozart's operas? Recognitions of persons do occur and with some frequency, but they do not usually reveal close blood ties. When they do, as in the case of *Idomeneo,* they do not necessarily hold the privileged position with respect to the overall action that reading Aristotle might lead us to expect. Indeed, the examples we have considered here suggest that, because the recognition that reveals close blood ties is not dominant, the new paradigm conceives of the individual as a more independent figure in society, one whose actions are not governed by his or her family identity. Recognition is thus redirected toward the gaining of knowledge and affirming of contemporaneous values. In *Entführung,* as we have seen, the family recognition has actually been rejected by librettist and composer, who substitute a recognition scene of an entirely different kind in its place.

This is not to say that the simple recognition of identity cannot play a crucial role in the drama of a Mozart opera, only that the role it most often plays is not the one Aristotle imagined. Not surprisingly, the operas of the late eighteenth century on the one hand, and the plays of antiquity on the other, reflect very different cultures, separated by more than two thousand years, and dramatize very different kinds of themes. While Greek tragedy tends to be oriented toward family relationships and discoveries of individual identity, whatever other knowledge or new understanding the discovery may bring, Mozart's operas are oriented toward the Enlightenment precepts of relationships within society (marriage, rulership, membership, and so on). In this context, love and its social and moral confirmation in marriage take precedence over birthright. (In contrast, one cannot help but remember that it is the discovery of his birthright that *undoes* Oedipus's marriage.) Even where familial relationships exist, then, the fact of the relationship is not necessarily of paramount importance. In *Idomeneo,* as we have seen, the early discovery of family ties is eclipsed by later and more important discoveries of relationships within society: Idomeneo's recognition of the kind of ruler he should have been, the realization of Idamante's and Ilia's affection, and Neptune's benevolent decree that the happy couple shall rule over Crete. With the passing of old to new, the self-interest of Idomeneo's vow gives way to the more important late eighteenth-century concern for the common good. The opera dramatizes a shift from inherited wisdom and faith in gods to self-reliance and human truth. The plots of Mozart's operas might be thought to have been created on the cusp of this change, melding issues of family identity and status with the emerging Enlightenment concern for the beliefs, feelings, and human potential of the individual.

Disguise and Its Discovery

Recognition brought about by the removal of disguise, like other kinds of recognition, may be incidental or vital to its plot—and of little or great thematic significance—depending on how it is prepared and worked out. This sort of recognition, however, in which hidden identities are simply revealed once cloaks, hats, moustaches, spectacles, and other impediments to discovery have been removed, has often been thought of as a jaded convention. And those subplots most dependent on such artifice are often criticized as weak aspects of their respective dramas.

Take, for example, the episode in which master and servant switch cloaks and hats in act 2 of *Don Giovanni*. The imbroglio deepens and several new complications arise, but this entire series of scenes, which concludes when the two would-be seducers meet again in the cemetery, might be thought tangential to the larger plot. As a result, though not only for this reason, one often reads that the second act of this opera is far less well constructed than the first. But the unmasking of disguise, even in this case, is more complex than it might at first seem. It is of some consequence to the plot to see the servant dressed up as the master; indeed it is a fulfillment of the wish Leporello expressed in the *introduzione*, "Voglio far il gentil uomo" (I would like to be the gentleman). In the event, however, Leporello proves unable to play the part of Don Giovanni. When confronted by his master's accusers in the sextet No. 19, he gladly reveals himself. It is difficult to imagine that the experience of disguise and discovery moves Leporello, a character little given to reflection, to any profound realization, but the episode draws an important contrast between servant and master. While Don Giovanni wears his disguise easily, Leporello does not. While Don Giovanni stands up to and outwits his human adversaries, Leporello cannot. At the same time, while Don Giovanni will die for his crimes, Leporello will not.

Even when it appears to be an unnecessary contrivance, disguise often proves important to the psychological development and motivations of the characters as well as to the design and preparation of the plot. The opening of *Don Giovanni* illustrates how disguise may facilitate the drama in a special way, for it is quite clear that Don Giovanni would not have attacked Donna Anna—and in her father's house—without the cover of a mask. The events that ensue during the *introduzione*, then, engender the entire action of the opera. But the mask itself, in this case, is quite transparent. The fact that Don Giovanni is a ruthless libertine, one who will try to force a woman if he cannot persuade her, is finally more central to his story than the fact of his name or his noble heritage or his position in the society of Seville. He thus appears to be more himself in the *introduzione* with his mask on than he appears in the street scene later in act 1 when he greets Donna Anna and Don Ottavio with his mask off. Indeed, he has betrayed these social marks of identity with his actions, which are unmasked long before he is.

Disguise is a stock device of comedies, of course, and common to the opera buffa of Mozart's day. Paisiello's *Il barbiere di Siviglia* and *Il re Teodoro in Venezia* and also Haydn's *Il mondo della luna* are familiar examples, but there are many others. I use the term "disguise" in this context to designate the act of consciously concealing identity. For the purposes of this discussion, the use of veils in *Zauberflöte*, the madness of Violante and Count Belfiore in *Giardiniera*, the pastoral existence of the shepherd king in *Il re pastore* who does not know his true identity, and other episodes involving hidden, changed, or uncertain identity, while surely related, are not considered examples of disguise. In the service of farce, a mask may conceal identity and nothing more. In Mozart, however, recognition scenes that center on uncovering a disguise often bring about a new understanding of circumstances or even an entirely new situation. In Mozart's operas, as in Shakespeare's comedies, the removal of the mask reveals the familiar in a new aspect. That which was known is discovered and *recovered*, and in the process a new significance is recognized and new understanding achieved. That the Da Ponte operas center to such a degree on disguise is perhaps borne of the fact that these works are Mozart's most complex multiple-plot comedies, examples of a genre in which disguise is a common device.

It might be thought that recognitions involving disguise constitute a special case, but they appear to function with as much variability and unpredictability as other recognitions of persons. And, like the examples we explored in the previous section, recognitions of persons that depend on disguise often privilege not merely the discovery of identity but the discoveries of other kinds that are either made possible by it or are attendant upon it. The crux of *Giardiniera*, for example, turns on the identity of the "pretend" garden girl. The discovery that Sandrina is really the Marchesa Violante, however, does not halt the action but rather propels it forward toward the later and more important discoveries of mutual affection and reconciliation among several parties. Even at the close of the opera, questions of identity raised by the fact of disguise remain: What does it mean to be a "pretend" garden girl? Why does this particular disguise facilitate the drama in ways others would not? Disguise itself is often the sign of a deeper recognition, waiting to be brought to the surface. Though disguise may conceal the identity of persons who would otherwise be recognized, the revelation made when the disguise is removed typically uncovers more than merely the identity hidden behind the mask.

For example, in the act 4 finale of *Figaro*, the Count pursues a woman he believes to be Susanna (Susanna and her mistress have switched dresses, just as Leporello and his master switched cloaks) but who is in fact the Countess in disguise. When, at the